James S. Norris, during his twenty-five-year career on Madison Avenue in New York, participated in the marketing efforts behind many products. He is currently a professor of marketing at Florida Junior College in Jacksonville, Florida, and has written three textbooks on marketing published by Prentice-Hall, Inc., and Reston Publishing Co. He is also self-employed as a marketing consultant and market researcher, and he specializes in small, local business and in new business ventures.

HOW TO WIN IN BUSINESS

A Guide to Effective Marketing

JAMES S. NORRIS

A SPECTRUM BOOK

PRENTICE-HALL, INC., Englewood Cliffs, N.J. 07632

8-29-95

Library of Congress Cataloging in Publication Data

Norris, James S., 1915–
  How to win in business.

  "A Spectrum Book."
  Bibliography: p.
  Includes index.
  1. Marketing. I. Title.
  HF5415.N68 1983   658.8   83–15952
  ISBN 0–13–439554–9
  ISBN 0–13–439547–6 (pbk.)

ISBN 0-13-439554-9

ISBN 0-13-439547-6 {PBK.}

For Libby

Editorial/production supervision by Louise M. Marcewicz
Cover design by Jeannette Jacobs
Manufacturing buyer: Doreen Cavallo

© 1983 by Prentice-Hall, Inc., Englewood Cliffs, New Jersey 07632

A SPECTRUM BOOK

1   2   3   4   5   6   7   8   9   10

Printed in the United States of America

This book is available at a special discount when ordered
in bulk quantities. Contact Prentice-Hall, Inc., General
Publishing Division, Special Sales, Englewood Cliffs, N. J. 07632.

Prentice-Hall International, Inc., *London*
Prentice-Hall of Australia Pty. Limited, *Sydney*
Prentice-Hall of Canada Inc., *Toronto*
Prentice-Hall of India Private Limited, *New Delhi*
Prentice-Hall of Japan, Inc., *Tokyo*
Prentice-Hall of Southeast Asia Pte. Ltd., *Singapore*
Whitehall Books Limited, *Wellington, New Zealand*
Editora Prentice-Hall do Brasil Ltda., *Rio de Janeiro*

Contents

Introduction

This book was written with many people in mind—some of whom I know:

> Jim, who watched a new, interesting business fold its tents and silently steal away.
>
> Al, who has recently retired from the Navy and now finds himself in a world he never knew existed.
>
> Florence, bright, assertive, motivated mother of four who can't wait to put one career behind her and get started on another.

There are many, many more I have never met. But they are out there. . . .

"Marketing isn't just for marketers anymore" isn't simply a take-off on the orange juice slogan. The fact of the matter is that a knowledge of the fundamentals of marketing is important—if not essential—to almost everyone in business today.[1]

---

[1] See, for example, Kenneth J. Albert, *Straight Talk About Small Business* (McGraw-Hill, 1981), p. 29. The author points out that "companies that are founded without an emphasis on proper marketing are almost sure to fail."

Nor is marketing the exclusive province of big business. The pizza parlor on the corner has the same fundamental marketing problems as General Foods. The principles of marketing can be put to work just as effectively for a charitable organization, a politician, or a Little Theatre as they were for Adidas sports equipment.

This book explains what it takes to construct a successful marketing plan from A to Z. It is logically arranged, for you to learn in small doses. It isn't a college textbook, and you'll find it easy and fun to read. When you have finished studying it, you will know *all* the marketing moves made by those who win in business. Good luck!

1

What Marketing
Is All About

HOW TO GET YOUR HANDS
ON THE WHEEL

Exchanges of goods and services have been taking place from the time one person had something to trade for something he or she valued more highly. Archeologists have found records of marketing transactions on clay tablets dating back thousands of years.

In the old port cities of the Mediterranean we can still find the traces of harbors, warehouses, and shops built by busy Greek and Roman merchants. Sailors braved the unknown seas to discover new trade routes. Columbus, Vasco da Gama, Magellan, and others opened up new markets in Africa, India, and the Orient.

From the seventeenth century to the twentieth, hardly a war was fought, whether in Canada, the Congo, China, or the West Indies, that was not fought to secure markets.

This is all ancient history, of course. Today, businesspeople still fight for markets, but they are much more likely to compete with new products, attractive trade discounts, and intensive promotion.

Modern marketing is a relatively recent development. In fact, until the 1930's few colleges even taught the subject. Since 1900 marketing has changed dramatically in clearly identifiable steps.

The Craftsman's Era

The necessities of life—food, fuel, fabrics—have always been marketed. But from earliest times it was the craftsman who could *execute* who rose to the top. Whether creating cathedrals, armor, jewelry, or musical instruments, his skills rendered his marketing problems simple ones.

This demand for fine craftsmanship has never died away completely. It is still present in our markets today, particularly in expensive luxury items.

The Mass Production Era

The moment a steam engine was harnessed to machinery and the Industrial Revolution started, it became possible to make *quantities* of a product. A steam-driven loom could make more cloth in a week than a person could weave in a winter. All kinds of new automatic machines were invented. It was now possible to make replaceable parts and to put them together on an assembly line.

The mass production era not only created more products, but also created a growing class of people with money to buy these products. This came about with the move of workers to the cities and the factories for better salaries.

As America expanded, markets and eager buyers expanded, too. Competing manufacturers raced to make more and sell more. The emphasis was on sales—moving the product.

The Marketing Era

The depression of the 1930s closed many of the over-expanded companies. The very maturing of America changed the face of the marketplace. Customers began to see products from different perspectives. Companies began to change their perspectives, too; they became satisfiers of needs, rather than vendors of products. They began to see their businesses in a different way, not as rug manufacturers, but as home beautifiers; not as makers of motorcycles, but as providers of freedom and excitement and transportation.

The Modern Marketing Concept

A concept may be regarded as a basic idea made up of contributing ideas. These contributing ideas differ quite radically from those that marketers followed up to just a few years ago. You will see the differences immediately.

MODERN MARKETING THOUGHT BEGINS WITH THE CONSUMER. As you see, we make a full circle: The marketing effort aims toward the ultimate purchasing decision of the consumer. It *begins* with consideration of what that decision might be. A company does not make a product first and then try to induce you to buy it. Rather, modern marketers determine your needs, wants, and aspirations and seek to provide the products that will satisfy them.

Sometimes the needs are as obvious as bread. Sometimes they must be assumed. "I'll bet if we made a board with a fin on it, there are lots of people who would enjoy the excitement and sport of riding waves with them." Or, "Why don't we put panty hose in egg-shaped containers and make them available from self-help display racks in supermarkets? I'll bet lots of women would like the convenience of buying stockings that way."

MODERN MARKETING GETS EVERYONE INTO THE ACT. Production no longer regards its responsibilities as ending at the shipping room door. Nor does the sales department take the traditional attitude, "We don't care what you make. Just give it to us and we'll sell it." Each department has its designated part to play, and each department works with the others to achieve the ultimate marketing goal.

MODERN MARKETERS PLAN FOR PROFIT. Marketing plans are made with the profit possibilities well in mind—*not* ever greater volume. As you will see later on, it is quite possible to go broke by making too much.

MODERN MARKETING CONSIDERS THE COMMUNITY. The modern marketer regards himself or herself as a member of the community, with all of the social responsibilities that implies. The modern marketing company is concerned about the consumer. Therefore, it is very concerned about its *image* in the eyes of the consumer.

For instance, Texaco does not wish you to think of it as a company that spills oil all over the beaches. And Anheuser Busch is not too happy when one of their Budweiser cans lands in someone's front yard.

4

YOUR BLEND—AND HOW TO BREW IT

Some people go "marketing" with a market basket over their arms and a shopping list in their hands. Others visit a "market" such as the food store. But the marketing we will be talking about is different. It is a *process*.

A process *proceeds*. Thus, in marketing we proceed from the first glimmer of an idea for a product (or a service) until someone buys it and uses it. These two points *and everything in between* (other than the physical production process) is of interest to us in the study of marketing. Hence, we might say that marketing is *a process by which goods and services find their way from the seller to the buyer.*

One way to explore what happens when goods and services are proceeding from seller to buyer or from maker to user is to study the process of one product. It turns out that those attractive new slacks of yours traveled an interesting journey. Let's look at it.

Factors the Marketer Can Control

There were a number of stages before your slacks came to you. We can identify quite clearly those over which the manufacturer had control.

1. The manufacturer made decisions regarding the design, the quality of the fabric, and the kind of workmanship that would go into the slacks.

2. The manufacturer worked out a price that would be charged for them.

3. The manufacturer's salespeople set up outlets—both retail stores and wholesale distributors.

4. The manufacturer developed a plan to promote, through advertising and other means, this line of slacks to wholesalers, retailers, and people like you.

5. A way to package the slacks was decided upon. On a special hanger? In a printed plastic sack?

These five factors, you will notice, involved *decisions* on the part of the manufacturer and his or her associates—the controllables we keep talking about.

The Marketing Mix

These five decisions, regarding *product, price, distribution, promotion,* and *packaging* must be made by anyone who creates something he or she hopes people will buy.

These five elements are blended together in a mix that the maker thinks will bring victory in the marketplace. Moreover, each blend is unique to each manufacturer. Just as the blenders of a Scotch whiskey cherish their particular formula and just as Colonel Sanders won't tell anyone what goes into his fried chicken batter, so the manufacturer creates a marketing mix in an individual way.

Factors the Marketer Can't Control

Life, as you have no doubt observed, is full of uncertainties. There are surprises, too, as your slacks proceed on their way from market to you. The manufacturer wishes this was not so. He keeps his fingers crossed and hopes for the best, but there is not much he or she can do about these things.

1. *Style, tastes, fads.* For the manufacturers of men's and women's fashions this is indeed a risky factor. Who knows whether six months from now you and your friends will wear only straight-legged slacks or prefer bell-bottoms? What new interest such as jogging will sweep the country, resulting in millions of dollars of sales in running shoes, warm-up suits, and even books on jogging? Why do people suddenly go one way—and then suddenly go another?

2. *Laws and regulations.* There are many laws and regulations governing the way people do business. The ways a product is made, priced, packaged, promoted, and distributed are all subject to regulation. The marketer must market *within* the law.

3. *The economy.* You can bet that every marketer keeps a close watch on the economy. He or she wants to know how much disposable income you have, whether you have a job, what the interest rates are, and how easy it is to borrow money.

These factors and others are going to affect the product as it proceeds from the seller's control to the buyer's. This is one of the major reasons why marketing directors are interested in forecasting. These uncontrollable factors are often referred to as the *marketing environment.*

What is Marketing?

I think you may safely say, based on what you have learned and what you experienced, that marketing is a process in which . . .

1. A manufacturer makes a pair of slacks and

2. creates a plan involving quality, price, distribution, promotion, and packaging, which will operate under whatever environmental conditions exist

3. all to the end that *someone* will buy these slacks, put them on, and wear them with a great deal of satisfaction.

Note that it was *someone* who bought the slacks. Note also that he or she is the end of the line—the culmination and climax of the whole marketing process. The success or failure of the whole marketing program hangs on the consumer's decision to buy or not to buy. If they (in their hundreds of thousands) have . . .

1. Decided slacks are out of style,
2. Dislike the cut,
3. Find the price too high,
4. Have never heard of this particular brand,
5. Can't find them in their favorite store, or
6. Aren't attracted by the way they are packaged

. . . then they will make a decision—and that decision is likely to be thumbs down!

WE ARE ALL SOMEONE'S SLICE OF THE PIE

But what if I have never worn a pair of slacks—and never intend to? Wouldn't you be wasting your time and money trying to sell to me? You sure would! The fact is, there is hardly a product you can name that doesn't have "never-never" buyers. You probably know a lot of people who are *never* going to buy a Rolls-Royce or dentures or panty hose or a tractor-pulled lawn-cutter.

By the same token, there are many people who *are* quite possibly going to buy your product. They have all the qualifications—

money, good-looking legs, or a three-acre lawn. These people are called a *target market*. We will only aim for these consumers.

You can make a diagram of this. Let your market (hometown or senior citizens, for example) be represented by a circle. Each target market can be represented by a segment of that circle—a slice of the pie, so to speak. The slice representing the Rolls Royce target market will be very narrow, indeed. But the slice for bath soap will be quite large since nearly everyone takes a bath. But if the product is mechanics hand soap for removing grease and grime, again, the slice will be small.

We call these slices *market segments*. The process of dividing up a market is called *market segmentation*.

... AND EVERY SLICE HAS A DIFFERENT LOOK

It is of paramount importance that you understand the concept of segmentation. One of the biggest reasons for business failure—particularly *new* business failure—is that the managers do not realize that they have a segment which is their target market. They have not identified it.

Every target market has a definite look of its own. Its appearance should be as familiar to you as the face in your mirror—every wart, wrinkle, and blemish. The characteristics of a target market is called a *market profile*. In Chapter 6 you will see in detail how one develops a market profile.

First, however, we are going to take a closer look at customers —and what makes them behave the way they do.

2

The Way We Are:
Getting to Know
Your Customers

IF YOU DON'T UNDERSTAND ME,
HOW CAN YOU TALK TO ME?

As you have seen, the marketing process begins and ends with the consumer. As a matter of fact, there is very little in marketing that is not directly affected by the customer and his or her behavior.

Therefore, it is best that we understand all we can about the remarkable, unpredictable, fascinating customer. Our marketing success rests in his or her hands; everything we do in marketing is done in his or her shadow.

There is nothing new in consumer behavior. The rug merchant on the streets of ancient Bagdad knew when to plead and when to remain firm, when to laugh and when to cry. He _knew_ his customers. What modern salesperson does not pride himself or herself on an ability to size up a customer, read character, or apply a little psychology?

It is astonishing to read the famous and successful ads of the mass sellers of thirty years ago and to see how much they understood about human behavior and how to turn it to their benefit. Charles Atlas apparently knew something about the problems of adolescence and the 90-pound weakling. Listerine knew about the pains and fears of rejection. And people who sold mail-order language lessons to the girl who always ordered chicken salad in a French restaurant because she couldn't read the menu seemed to know *exactly* what they were doing.

However, only recently have we had logical explanations for much of this behavior. Past marketers learned what worked by trial and error. Today we are beginning to understand *why* these things work because we are beginning to understand much more about the human personality through the fast-developing science of behaviorism.

It all comes down to a very simple proposition: *If I do not understand you, I cannot expect you to understand me.* And if you do not understand me, then the whole marketing process comes to a grinding halt.

FAMILIES ARE MADE UP OF CHANGEABLE PARTS

Our buying behavior is influenced by the people we are closest to—our families and our friends. If you think for a moment, you can probably trace many of your purchasing decisions to those around you. Did you buy those attractive new boots after your best friend turned up in a similar pair? Did you get a lawn edger after watching your neighbor use one?

The Family Life Cycle

From the moment we are born, we are members of a family. Our position in that family strongly indicates the way we spend our money in stores or the way money is spent on us. Let us look at the life cycle and see how it influences spending.

SINGLES.   Relatively free of financial responsibilities, singles usually find they have available cash, and this is most often spent on fun products and services: cars and motorcycles, sporting goods, clothing, stereo equipment, vacations, and entertainment. Many get married, and their lives change radically.

THE NEWLYWEDS.   Newly married couples are likely to be comfortable financially; often both partners work. But their expenditures are high, too. Many of their purchases will be home furnishings and other durable goods. Usually they are fashion conscious and spend liberally on clothes. They often will still spend on recreational equipment, too.

THE NEST.   As children come, the family spending pattern again alters drastically. From the obstetrician's bill through teeth straightening to college tuition, a youngster costs more every year. Though family income increases during these years, demands are greater. When the children are old enough, a parent who has been their primary caretaker often returns to work, increasing the family income. As time goes by, both husband and wife become more skilled and careful in their purchase decisions.

THE EMPTY NEST.   Another radical change takes place when the children are grown and have left home. Mothers and fathers suddenly find themselves with more disposable income and more leisure time. They are likely to spend more on vacations and new hobbies. They may even return to school or college. By now their home is a major investment, and repairs and improvements, long·delayed, are undertaken.

RETIREMENT.   At this stage, there is a sharp drop in income, with inflation squeezing many couples far more than they expected. The family home is sold and replaced by an apartment, often in another part of the country. Meals become much simpler, and the food budget is watched carefully. Medical expenses usually rise, and the druggist's bill certainly goes up. On the other hand, far less is spent on clothing. Informal dress is the rule, and generally it is discovered that there is still lots of wear in slacks and jackets that have been hanging in the closet for a long time.

Awareness of this life cycle is vital to marketing people. If you were to open a clothing store in College Station, Texas, or State College, Pennsylvania, you would certainly do your buying with a very definite group in mind.

KEEPING UP—AND DOWN—
WITH THE JONESES

People tend to have groups of friends whose tastes, attitudes, and patterns of behavior are much like their own. These groups are important to us. It gives us a warm, secure feeling to be a member of the crowd. But if one is a loner or an odd ball and insists on doing things one's own way, one may be rejected by the crowd. For some of us this can result in a very insecure feeling. For young people, this feeling leads them to do things they otherwise would not do in order to secure a place in their gang.

Absorbing Values

Very often the values and attitudes of the crowd become our values and attitudes. We absorb them and make them our own; we do what the group expects us to do.

When you meet the crowd at the tavern on Saturday night, you all probably order the same brand of beer. In fact, the whole social pattern of your life may be formed by the crowd. People who sell cosmetics and kitchenware at in-home parties well know the strength of group influence.

Opinion Leaders and Trend Setters

In every group there seems to be one person who exercises considerable influence on the ideas and actions of the rest of the group. Perhaps you know one. She's the woman who always seems to turn up first in the latest styles, or he's the fellow who gets the gang together and organizes a rugby club.

These trend setters are very important to us. We want very much for them to discover and adopt us, for this may be the road to popularity. When a new restaurant opens, the owner usually takes great pains to invite the right people—sports stars or social celebrities—for a free meal and drink. The owner hopes that these celebrities will bring their friends, who will in turn be followed by others who wish to be seen with celebrities.

Marketers frequently use opinion leaders in their advertisements: The wise lady from next door who knows just how to make a cup of coffee; the experienced druggist who is waiting for you to ask him about your dandruff problem.

Diffusion or "Trickle-Down" Theory

Marketers have been interested for some time as to how and how fast the trend setter's ideas and fancies get out to the rest of the public. One theory is that it occurs in steps from the mass media to the trend setters to the general public. Women's wear people say styles trickle down from the Paris originals bought by the wealthy and style conscious to the copies of those originals mass merchandised the next year.

Yet there seem to be too many exceptions to make it possible to fit everyone into neat percentage categories. Many people are resistant to innovations. Nor are opinion leaders necessarily trend setters. The trend toward hatlessness which began some years ago started with people in the theatre and on college campuses. People in the distilling industry will tell you that the switch from blends to straights, and later from straights to vodka, could first be detected in black communities.[1]

SURE YOU HAVE CLASS

Americans seldom think of themselves as belonging to one social class or another. We're all Americans. This country isn't like the old country where class distinctions are rigidly maintained, and where family and titles often dictate a person's place in society.

However, there are differences between us, and some are easy to detect. There are people in America who are poor, undereducated, and often unemployable. There are also others of great distinction, accomplishment, wealth, and social position.

In between is the great majority of people making up the middle class. This large middle class can be further subdivided into blue collar and white collar. The former includes all who work with their hands in mines and mills, on docks and ships and construction sites. The latter are people employed in offices, stores, and government jobs.

How Social Class is Determined

Income is but one of the factors taken into consideration in determining social class. Others commonly used are occupation, type of housing, place of residence, and education. Indeed, some sociologists measure us by the books we read and the kinds of recreation we enjoy.

---

[1] Based on personal experience. Seagram Distillers and National Distillers.

How Many in Each Class

One widely accepted estimate holds that 13% of Americans fall in the upper-upper, lower-upper, and upper-middle classes. (The latter is professionals and business executives.) Sixty-one percent of the population is in the white-collar and blue-collar middle classes while 25% are in the bottom class on the scale.[2]

Buying Behavior of Social Classes

Our social class makes a big difference to the people who want to sell us things. This is evidenced in many ways. Beer is traditionally a working class drink. Sure enough, commercials for Bud and Miller show men coming off the job and into the local bar—and they are always blue-collar workers. Brewers have long known that the average pub-drinking working man can consume more beer between 4 and 6 p.m. than the average homemaker takes home from the store in a month.

Different kinds of stores attract different kinds of people. There is an obvious social distinction between those who shop at Sears and those who patronize the best department store in town.

A person's position on the social scale is reflected in his or her choice of food, recreation, cars, and clothing. Hence, it is very important for marketers to recognize the influence of social class.

DID YOUR MOTHER COME FROM IRELAND?

Go through the phone book and pick out some names—Anderson, Assim, Bernardi, Casmanski, Davis, McGraw, Robicheux, Shofuofulo, Smith, Wong, Zinsser—why, our forebears came from all over the world! This makes our country an exciting and different one to live in; so many different subcultures have taken root and flourished here and made their contribution to the mainstream of American life. Wherever you may live—Pennsylvania Dutch country, Miami, San Francisco, or New Bedford, Massachusetts—the character of each city is shaped by the cultural background of the people who live there.

Think of some of the ways ethnics have influenced our way of

[2] W. Lloyd Warner, *American Life, Dreams and Reality* (Chicago: The University of Chicago Press, 1953).

living. You never attend a jazz concert without hearing the beat of a West African drum. I'm sure you know where your pizza comes from as well as the beer to wash it down. We attend the same churches, mosques, and synagogues our greatgrandparents did. On certain days we turn out by the thousands to march proudly behind the Polish falcon, the green harp of Ireland, or the shrill pipes of Scotland.

These differences among us in cultural background require understanding. *Not understanding* our neighbors had led to some costly and often funny errors. Chevrolet had to change the name of its Nova car to Carribe in Latin America: *no va* means "it doesn't go" in Spanish! If you plan to make a radio appeal to a predominantly young, black, male audience, you better watch what you say and how you say it.

3

Have You Heard About Bongo the Ape and His Bananas?

WHAT WE HAVE LEARNED
ABOUT LEARNING

In Chapter 2 we examined some of the important *outside* influences
that affect the way we act as consumers: our families, friends, and
forebears.

Now we are going to examine some of the things that go on
inside us and that certainly have just as great an influence on our
buying habits. Be careful; you may be in for some surprises! In our
progress toward understanding, we will be asking ourselves why did
we buy that stereo, those slacks, that automobile. The answers, in many
cases, may be astonishing.

Let us begin with something you are doing right now—learning. You cannot see learning. But you can see the results of learning;
you can see what I do as a result of having learned something. So we
can assume that learning took place. I took guitar lessons, and now I

can play the C, G, D, and F chords. I learned the chords. For this reason, psychologists define learning in terms of behavior capability: *learning is a process in which behavior capabilities are changed as a result of experience* (with certain exceptions).

Learning is very important to marketers. They want to teach you about a product or service so that you will behave in a certain way when the time comes to buy. They don't expect you to dash to the drugstore the moment you see their TV commercial. But later on, when you have a cold, they want their remedy to be the one that is foremost in your mind.

FIRST YOU GET THE MULE'S ATTENTION

As you know, it can be easy to forget things. The technical term for this is *extinction*. Marketers do not want you to forget their cold remedy so they do not run a commercial once and let it go at that. They keep repeating commercials so it will be difficult for you to forget them when you catch a cold.

Learning can't be seen. Therefore, one has to develop theories about how it works. Different psychologists have different theories about how learning takes place. Here are three of the major ones.

Stimulus-Response Theory

This theory states that we learn by associating one event with another. When a certain action (stimulus) occurs, we act in a certain way (response). The Russian physiologist Pavlov stressed this in his famous dog experiments. He demonstrated that when a bell was rung and a dog was given food, the dog's mouth would water. After this was repeated a number of times, the dog's mouth could be made to water with the sound of the bell *alone*. The dog had associated the ringing of the bell and food.

It also was clear from this experiment that the more often an event occurred (*repetition*) and the closer the experiments were together (*contiguity*), the more effective the learning process. Repetition and contiguity thus became two very important principles in learning.

We have seen how the cold remedy commercial is repeated so that it will be learned. But note that the commercial always shows the blessed relief that occurs when the remedy is used. This is the contiguity of reward that comes from having learned and acted correctly. In fact, if you watch advertising carefully you will note that a pleasant reward almost always is associated with the product: for the woman whose husband admires her coffee-making ability, for the homemaker whose friends admire the gloss on her furniture, for the party-goer who solves his morning-after problems by plopping a white tablet into a glass of water.

VIRTUE, THEY SAID, IS ITS OWN REWARD

Behavior Modification

This theory, often associated with psychologist B.F. Skinner, is called operant learning. Although there are many professionals who don't agree with this theory, it is widely accepted in the United States.

Behavior modification theory states that our behavior is controlled by the *consequences* of the behavior—rewards and punishments. Skinner showed that if a rat received an electric shock when it entered a certain area, it would learn to avoid that area. When the rat discovered that food would appear when a certain button was touched, it would learn to select that button.

As in stimulus-response, repetition, or *reinforcement,* plays a major part. Learning takes place most quickly when the reinforcement is *continuous.* But some kinds of reinforcement need only be *intermittent.* I attend Homecoming at my alma mater only once a year, but I enjoy the big game and all the hoopla just as much each time.

As you have seen in so many ads and commercials, this concept of rewards is basic to marketing. When you buy a product or service, you gain a reward in the form of satisfaction. As satisfaction follows satisfaction with continued use, we become committed to a product. It is not until another marketer can thoroughly convince us of even more satisfaction that we think of deserting it.

HOW TO ADD TWO AND TWO— AND GET SIX

Cognitive Learning

However, another school of theorists says that stimulus-response and behavior modification do not account for many evident aspects of learning. What about our ability to derive meanings, to perceive implications, to put two and two together and get six?

The theory of cognitive learning is usually associated with

Wolfgang Kohler and Gestalt psychology with its emphasis on problem-solving. It states that we are able to solve problems using insight, recognizing relationships among the elements of the problem.

Kohler's early experiments with apes showed insight at work in a dramatic fashion. A bunch of bananas was hung just out of the ape's reach. A box was also placed in the cage. The ape jumped for the bananas several times and could not reach them. He gave up and sat down. His eyes lit on the strange box in his cage, and he looked at it for awhile. Then the light dawned. He picked up the box, placed it under the bananas, climbed up on the box, and collected his reward! The ability to reach our goals through cognitive reasoning, just as the ape reached the bananas, is a fundamental of modern marketing.

Consumers seek to solve the problems of satisfying their needs. Therefore, it is up to us as marketers to show our customers how our product is going to accomplish this.

You can see this every day: the laundry detergent that solves "ring around the collar," the gasoline that fights fuel prices by giving more miles to the gallon, the car rental people who make it possible for you to step right off the plane and into your rental car without delay.

The modern marketer seeks to meet the goals, needs, and aspirations of the consumer.

4

How to Get
A Customer
From 0 to 60 M.P.H.
in 15 Seconds

THE IGNITION SWITCH—
AND WHERE TO FIND IT

If you don't know me, you can't sell to me. It's as simple as that. If you don't know me, you can't find me. You won't know what I like and dislike. You won't know my habits and hang-ups. You won't know how to talk to me. And there is a large number of other things that are going to make your job as salesperson very difficult.

In this chapter we will see how marketers get to know everything they can about the consumer.

The Market

Marketing people think of consumers in terms of markets. We, as a group, are usually a market for something. For instance, one market is all the people in the United States who use toothpaste. When you hear a toothpaste manufacturer talking about his *share of market,* he's talking about the group of people in the whole toothpaste market who buy his product.

Markets can be places, too. Thus, you will hear someone refer to the "Jacksonville market" or the "Pacific Northwest market." And just to make it a little more confusing, markets can be referred to in terms of types of people such as the "youth market" or the "Spanish-speaking market." Don't be concerned about this because, for the moment, we will talk only about the people-who-buy-things market.

MARKET SEGMENTS.   If you were to take a market such as your hometown and think of it as a big pie, you would see that many product manufacturers have a slice of that pie. The soap manufacturers have a big slice because almost everyone takes a bath. Rolls-Royce, however, may have a very tiny slice. Makers of women's hosiery have a very definite slice—just about 50% of the adult market.

THERE IS A MARKET FOR EVERYONE.   Or there had better be. Wise marketers make every effort to ensure that there are people who are likely to buy their product. For some products, particularly new ones, this can be very risky. It is best to do some very good market studies beforehand.

Fortunately, there are other markets you can be sure of. If you are a manufacturer of shaving cream, you know that just as sure as the alarm clock goes off tomorrow morning, there is a large number of men with beards to shave off. If you sell denture adhesive, you can be fairly certain that there will always be a certain number of people who neglected to see their dentists twice a year and have dentures.

Market Profiles

What do the consumers look like? How many of them are there and where can I find them? These are some of the things marketers want to know. As we said, if you don't know your customers, you can't sell to them.

Marketing managers have ways to measure their market segments. If they discover ten characteristics about a consumer, a picture begins to emerge, what we call a *profile.*

THE PARTS OF THE PROFILE.   There are ten commonly accepted measurements that we apply to a segment. Let's list them and comment briefly on each one.

1. *Income.* This is how much money you make and especially how much you have to spend (disposable income) after the rent, food, and payment on the car have been taken care of.

2. *Education.* Did you finish high school, college? What you know has a lot to do with your buying decisions.

3. *Sex.* Men and women often present entirely different kinds of markets.

4. *Age.* Your buying habits vary with your years.

5. *Religion.* With some products in some places, this is very important: New York City, Boston, Salt Lake City.

6. *Occupation.* Whether you are a steelworker or a college professor may say something about your buying habits.

7. *Location.* Where do you live?

8. *Ethnic Origin.* This is a particularly interesting one. We all have ethnicity to a certain extent. Many of us have tastes and habits brought to the United States by our ancestors from other parts of the world.

9. *Marital Status.* A married couple has a far different buying pattern from a single person—particularly if they are a family with children.

10. *Social Status.* Selling to blue-collar workers and to jetsetters often present very different problems.

HOW DO I FIND OUT ABOUT THESE PEOPLE? There are some very good sources to help you in drawing a market profile. For information on the preceding ten categories you can try these sources.

Census Reports. Every ten years, the U.S. Department of Commerce publishes *General Social and Economic Characteristics* for each state. Here you will find, broken down by counties and cities, practically all the basic statistical information on which marketers rely. If you want to know how many French- or Italian-speaking people there are in your county, it's there. How many families are below the poverty level or make over $50,000 a year? The Census has it.

"Survey of Buying Power." Published by Sales Management, this publication will show you figures for population breakdowns by age groups, heads of households by age, buying income, and cash income, and dollar retail sales for the past year in a variety of consumer categories (for example, drug, auto, clothing). The information is organized by marketing areas (Bridgeport, Stamford, Norwalk, Danbury, for example).

The Public Library and City Hall.   Many records are kept here which can be valuable to you—car registrations, electrical power turn-ons, and others.

Chamber of Commerce Research Director.   Usually only available to members, this source can be invaluable for local and regional information.

The Media.   This is one of the most productive and detailed sources of consumer information. Magazines, newspapers, and radio and TV stations are in the business of selling market segments—their listeners or readers. They know all about them.

HOW TO TURN PUSHES
INTO PROFITS

Motivation

Sounds like *motor*, doesn't it? We are now going to discuss what turns the customer on to your product. What gets his motor running and heads him for the product or service you have to sell?

To sell to you successfully, I must know many things about you, not just where you are and how much money you make and what your taste in soft drinks might be. I also need to understand the *forces* that influence your buying decisions, particularly as they concern my product.

The Influence of Friends
and Neighbors

Do you remember how important it was for you to follow the gang when you were a kid? If you had a bike, it had to be a Schwinn. You wouldn't think of wearing anything but bleached-out Levi jeans because that's what all your friends wore.

The same thing holds when we become adults. If one guy on the block gets a power lawn mower, soon everyone has to have a power lawn mower. Sometimes it takes a lot of courage and self-confidence to be a maverick.

Leaders And Style Setters

Often we play follow-the-leader when it comes to buying things. Of course, you've seen how this works. If the opinion leaders dictate that computer games are "in" this season, that's what every family in town will soon be playing. Nothing makes a restaurant owner happier than to have his place become the popular spot where sport stars gather. Trend setters can sometimes make a place or a product popular overnight.

The Kind of Life Style You Follow

Social status was already mentioned as one of the measurements used in preparing a market profile. Though social scientists divide us into categories such as upper class and middle class, the lines between us sometimes become blurred. What is important is the kind of life a person follows. Are you a beer drinker by preference, or do you usually have wine with dinner? How important is it to you and your neighbors that you keep your lawn neat and well-trimmed?

WHAT CUSTOMERS DON'T ALWAYS TELL THEIR ANALYSTS

Our natural needs and desires are often satisfied through the products and services we buy. For example, it's not very hard to sell you a box of Kentucky Fried Chicken when you are hungry. We all want to be admired and looked up to, which affects the kind of clothes we buy. In fact, a salesman can tell you what he sells isn't half as important as the benefits it provides. A person buys a mouthwash not only to have pleasant breath, but also to avoid the pain of social rejection. Boys buy and use barbells not just to get strong, but to gain the status of manhood and masculinity that goes along with bulging muscles.

Sometimes, because we don't recognize our personal needs and desires, we don't even know they are at work. Did you buy your newest slacks because you needed a pair of pants or because you wanted to look good and feel good?

Psychologists have defined some of these needs and desires. They say that there are needs and desires having to do with our bodies or natural functions such as needs for protection or food or sex. Then there are those that have to do with our emotions and personalities. These are such things as our need to have love and affection; our need to have self-respect, as well as the respect of others; our need to feel that we are doing a good job, getting a lot out of life, and doing what we want to do.

WHEN THE BUYER FEELS GOOD— YOU FEEL GOOD

When you are denied any of the needs mentioned previously, whether food or respect or love, you *hurt*. You want to relieve your pain. If my product will do that for you, then it is up to me to tell you so. The boy who sent away for the piano lessons by mail didn't just want to be able to play a pretty tune. What he *really* wanted was the affection and respect of his friends and the good feeling that comes with having worked hard and accomplished something.

There are many things that make us behave the way we do. Some of them are easy to see and some of them aren't so easy. Some stem from deep-seated psychological needs that we can't understand or aren't aware of. Others are as simple and understandable as keeping up with the Joneses. If you are going to market successfully, you must know all you can about behavior. Without that insight, you are at a terrible disadvantage.

HOW TO CLIMB THE LADDER NAMED DESIRE

Behavioral scientists have provided theories and research to explain why people act the way they do. One of the best known behavioral scientists is Dr. Abraham Maslow, whose famous hierarchy of needs and wants is quoted in many texts on advertising, salesmanship, or management as well as marketing.

Maslow (1954) developed a list of seven basic human needs and stated them in the order of their importance and priority. They are:

1. The normal bodily needs which must be satisfied for survival such as hunger, warmth, and protection.
2. The need for security from danger and the threats of danger.
3. The need to feel loved and to love others.
4. The need to be respected by others and to respect oneself.
5. The need to feel that one is working and achieving up to one's capability; the need to be one's best self.
6. The need to understand oneself and others.
7. The need to know and experience beauty and serenity.

The principles espoused by the social scientists have been adopted by many marketers, including Martineau (1957) and Dichter (1964). They have demonstrated how a knowledge of the human personality and behavior is necessary to successful marketing. A look at some of the great advertising of the past will provide you with a wealth of examples of how sellers appealed to the satisfaction of our basic needs. "They Laughed When I Sat Down at the Piano," "Often a Bridesmaid, Never a Bride," and "Again She Ordered Chicken Salad" are among the many whose appeals went directly to our needs for affection, respect, or security.

5

How to Unconfuse Yourself With Facts

In the last chapter, the formation of target markets was covered. The next natural step is for the marketer to ask questions about the look of the target market: Who are these individuals? Where do they live? How many of them are there? How much money do they have to spend?

The answer to these questions require the determination of facts. Until marketers have all the facts they do not move, because they do not know which way to move. Furthermore, there are quite a few questions in addition to these your marketer might also like to have answered.

For example, if you had saved and borrowed $50,000 in order to open a music store, what are some of the facts you'd like to know before you spent a penny of that hard-to-come-by cash? You'd want to know how many people you might serve and what their interests are in music. Should you stock sheet music as well as records and tapes? What kind of music does your market prefer—rock, jazz, classical? How well established are other music stores in your market? Once you get started—and remember, it's *your* money—one question follows another and the list of questions grows and grows.

This, then, is what the modern marketer is concerned with: *getting the answers to the questions.* Now we are going to examine the ways that you can gather the information that will help you to operate with the greatest chances of success.

Research—never leave home without it.

IT ISN'T WHAT YOU KNOW— IT'S KNOWING WHERE TO FIND IT

First, let us examine the facts you as a businessperson are most likely to seek. You will want to know about:

THE CUSTOMERS.   Who are you selling to? What do these individuals look like, and where do they live? How much money do they have to spend? What are their tastes and habits? These people are your target market, and you want to zero in on them.

THE PRODUCT.   Is it new or different? Does it have a competitive edge? Do people like the way it tastes or works? Are there others like it on the market, and at what price? Are you capable of manufacturing it? Do you have the kind of retailers and wholesalers who would be interested in handling it? Can it replace an older product in your product line?

THE PROMOTION.   How much money should you put behind this product? Where should you place your advertising? Should you use radio, TV, newspapers, magazines—and in what proportion? How much impact do your promotional efforts have on sales?

THE PRICE.   How are you going to position this product with regard to price? What market are you seeking to attract, and what can they be expected to pay? What profit structure should you set up for your company and your resellers?

THE DISTRIBUTION.   Where do you wish to sell? What kinds of stores do you wish to be in? Who will handle your warehousing and distribution? What part will shipping costs play in your profit structure?

THE PACKAGING.   Of all the package designs you have looked at, which is most appealing to the consumer? What are the possibilities in new packaging materials? Is there marketing potential in new shapes or sizes?

THE BUSINESS.   Are you ready to expand your line? Would an investment in research and development be worthwhile? Should you change your shipping and discount policies? What kinds of resellers do you want to cultivate?

THE SALES.   Are territories and individual salespeople meeting their quotas? Are you maintaining your share of the market versus competitors? What sales and promotional activities are your competitors planning? What new sales territories might be opened?

These are only a few kinds of questions you may want to answer. Many answers can be found within your organization: sales and production figures, prices, and market shares. You may have to go outside the organization for others: consumer relations, marketing opportunities, changes in tastes and attitudes.

This gathering of information from *inside* and *outside* the firm is known as *marketing research*. A more formal definition is provided by the Committee on Definitions of the American Marketing Association: "The systematic gathering, recording, and analyzing of data about problems relating to the marketing of goods and services." They point out that this systematic gathering may be done by the business itself or by impartial agencies (companies that specialize in performing marketing research projects). Such companies are the outside part of the process. The business is the inside.

Researchers distinguish between *research projects* which are set up to give answers to specific questions or problems and *research systems* which regularly return, analyze, and store needed information, from both inside and outside sources, so that it is available to marketing management. The latter is known as a *Marketing Information System* (M.I.S.). Please note, however, that whatever the source, it is all marketing information.

WHO TO ASK—WHAT TO ASK— HOW TO ASK

Just as "who, what, when, and where" guide the newspaper reporter in writing a story, so the market-information gatherer adheres to four broad principles in gathering marketing facts. Market researchers are concerned with *kind, form, accuracy*, and *timeliness* of the facts they gather.

MARKETING INFORMATION MUST BE SELECTIVE.   You cannot supply information about everything. No one would read it. A marketing director can only pay attention to selected information; anything else is a waste of his or her time.

MARKETING INFORMATION MUST BE CONCISE.   "The facts, ma'am, just the facts!" as the TV detective used to say. Keep it brief and to the point. The President of the U.S. doesn't read all the newspapers every morning, but he does read a concise summary prepared by his staff.

MARKETING INFORMATION MUST BE ACCURATE.   False or misleading information can be worse than no information at all. However, rumors, when labeled as such, often play an important role in marketing information.

MARKETING INFORMATION MUST BE TIMELY.   In today's fast-moving, fast-changing world, yesterday's facts can become very stale very quickly. Computers and data processing have created an information revolution. If you have ever stood at an airline counter and watched the clerk ask whether there's a seat on the next flight to Dallas and get the answer in a matter of seconds, you have seen how our information exchange systems have speeded up.

Sources Of Information—Inside

It has already been stated that marketing researchers gather useful information both *inside* and *outside* of the firm. Now sources for this information will be described. First, inside sources will be discussed.

SALES REPORTS.   If the company is national in scope, this may include summaries of sales by regions, share-of-market reports, sales by types of products, and comparative figures, quarterly or monthly. For a small store, it might be as simple as the answer to, "How did we do last week?"

INVENTORY REPORTS.   "How much of each product do we have on hand?" In many businesses, the company's reputation for service may depend on the correct answer to this question.

CREDIT REPORTS.   "Does this customer pay his bills on time?" "How much does he owe us?" This information is sometimes vital if the company is to avoid losses.

PROFIT-AND-LOSS STATEMENTS.   Just as the figures in the company's published annual report, these financial statements give management a quick overview of the company's financial status at any time.

It is obvious how helpful it can be to have a computer terminal in the office. This information is then literally at your fingertips within a few moments of your requesting it.

Sources Of Information—Outside

In addition to the facts and figures available to you within your own company, other sources of information are readily available to you.

CENSUS OF POPULATION—GENERAL SOCIAL AND ECONOMIC CHARACTERISTICS.   The U.S. Department of Commerce publishes these volumes every ten years by each state. They contain basic demographic information: occupation, income, social characteristics, and so on.

STATISTICAL ABSTRACT OF THE U.S.   Published yearly by the U.S. Department of Commerce, this volume contains the figures on a wide variety of government and business activities.

MOODY'S INDUSTRIAL MANUAL.   Published yearly by Moody's Investor's Service, Inc., this source gives the basic facts on all U.S. companies issuing stocks or bonds.

In addition to the above basic sources, there are:

THE PUBLIC LIBRARY.   The business section of your library is a storehouse of business information. Business directories, financial statements, and national advertisers and their agencies are but a few of them. Tell the librarians what you need and they will probably put it in your hand in no time at all.
Some secondary sources you will most likely find very useful are the Business Periodicals Index (a listing of all articles that have appeared in business publications) and other indexes that cover professional fields, medicine, or engineering. The New York Times Index is

also an excellent source of information because it covers the news for the record, often reprinting speeches in their entirety. There are also biographical indexes.

THE CHAMBER OF COMMERCE.   It helps to be a member, of course. Most chambers have a research director who is a great source of local business information. Often he or she can give you the information you need over the phone.

THE CITY HALL.   Tax, license, real estate, and utility information is available here. However, it is sometimes necessary to know the right person to go to. Experience has shown that a token remembrance in the holiday season can make your job a lot easier. A little something that says "I appreciate your help" is quite acceptable.

TRADE ASSOCIATIONS.   If your business belongs to a trade association such as American Bankers or Paint and Hardware Dealers, you can call on your particular association to give you information, particularly if it pertains to your own business.

TRADE PUBLICATIONS.   Perhaps you aren't familiar with them yet, but there is a publication for practically any kind of business you can name. Whether you make perfume, raise Poland China hogs, fish for the commercial market, or raise honey bees, there is a publication for you. The editorial offices are great repositories of information, and they will be delighted to help you, particularly if you are an advertiser.

MARKET RESEARCH COMPANIES.   Organizations such as Starch, Gallup and Robinson, and A.C. Nielsen can provide marketing surveys to their subscribers. Perhaps you have heard of the Nielsen ratings on which the fate of your favorite TV show may hang; Nielsen also supplies regular share-of-market surveys to its subscribers.

The Research Study

RESEARCH FINDS NEW FACTS.   The kind of information we have just reviewed is already in existence. You simply have to go and dig it out. This kind of information is referred to as *secondary data*.

However, when you uncover facts that have not been uncovered and recorded before or when you go through your company's files and develop new facts, this new information is called *primary data*. Very frequently it is primary data that we need most desperately, to supplement our secondary data in arriving at the correct marketing decisions.

You can't go to a library and discover how many people pass a certain intersection within a certain time period. There are no figures as to whether the public will like the taste of your new cereal. You have to search and find out this information.

ORGANIZING FOR RESEARCH.   Obtaining primary data is one of the most vital—and difficult—aspects of marketing. The approach to organizing this search for information follows. As we go along, some companies that either didn't bother to do research at all or who did it wrong will be discussed.

What's the Problem?   Knowing what you want to know is not always as easy or obvious as it may seem. You might think that you are seeking the answer to, "Would this be a good location for a fast-food place?" What you *should* be asking is, "How many working mothers pass by this location between 5 and 7 p.m.?"

You see, you can get the answer to this question quite quickly and accurately. The more *specific* the question, the easier it is to get the answer.

Sometimes we mistake *symptoms* for problems. A soft drink bottler may feel that his slipping sales represent a problem. Actually, they represent a symptom of a problem. The real problem is the fact that a certain percentage of the market finds the taste of his drink less acceptable than those of his competitors. Now *that* is something we can determine with considerable accuracy through research.

The Situational Analysis.   Finding out what the true problem is and what the right questions should be sometimes requires a great deal of preliminary work on the part of researchers. Often the process is like a detective sifting through every possible clue. Like detectives, the researchers probe and question a variety of people, following down every promising lead. Sometimes it requires patient, time-consuming checking of records and reports. In the case of our soft drink bottler researchers might question many people—retailers, customers, truck jobbers—until they begin to zero in on the problem, the taste.

Note that these researchers for the fast food store and the soft drink firm could not turn to an established source such as a library or chamber of commerce for the needed information because it has not been recorded anywhere. They had to search for and find it themselves. They were gathering primary data.

Building a Research Project
Without Pain—Or $50,000

A research project has four steps that must be carried out precisely and accurately. A misstep at any one of the four stages can destroy the validity of the whole study. The four steps are:

1. Selecting the people from whom you wish to receive answers—the *respondents*.
2. Deciding on the *manner* in which you wish to question them.
3. Putting into precise language the *questions* you wish to ask them.
4. *Analyzing and interpreting* what they tell you.

Let us consider, now, these four steps and see what it takes to perform each one properly:

1. THE SAMPLE. If we wish to find out about preferences in beer, we cannot ask every beer drinker in town. It would cost too much and take too long. So we take a *sample* of the beer drinkers. Just as a nurse takes a few cc's of blood to represent an entire blood supply, so we select a relatively small group of people who will be representative of the whole.

Types of Samples. Researchers recognize two types of samples: *probability* and *nonprobability*. A nonprobability sample is one with its members selected *purposefully*, not at random. An example of a nonprobability sample is a panel of homemakers selected and retained by a food manufacturer to provide input on how homemakers in general (the universe, in this example) might react to his food product.

A *probability* sample is one that is selected at *random* from the relevant universe—that is, in a manner in which every unit has an equal chance of being selected. For instance, you might take the phone book and from every third column, select every tenth name.

A *stratified* sample is one which reflects the make-up of your group. We restrict the sample members by grouping them according to some common characteristic. We then select specific numbers by random means from the groups. For instance, in your town the population may be 60% women and 40% men. To get meaningful results, your sample must truly reflect the make-up of the entire town. Therefore, your sample would consist of 60% women and 40% men, randomly selected. If you questioned a sample that consisted of 75% men and 25% women, it might throw your results off because it would be *weighted* or skewed (as researchers call it) in favor of men.

2. THE METHOD OF QUESTIONING.   There are four methods of questioning your respondents, each of which has built-in advantages and disadvantages.

By Telephone.   Telephone interviews must be brief and to the point. For example, "What television show are you watching?" But, telephone interviews are inexpensive to make and since they are brief many can be done in a short time.

By Mail.   Questionnaires sent through the mail to selected respondents can be long and detailed (*depth interviews*). But they are expensive since postage, printing, and handling are involved. In some cases, percentage returns may be low. But if they are sent to selected groups such as club members they will show a good rate of return and can supply a great deal of information.

By Personal Interview.   This method can be expensive, since trustworthy and experienced interviewers are required; many times the interviewer must be a trained psychologist who can frame questions properly and steer the interview in the most productive way. But excellent *depth* can be achieved; respondents are often very cooperative with a polite and personable interviewer. Sympathetic and sensitive interviews often gain surprising insights.

Panels.   Groups of people, who may be specialists in their fields, are easily organized and need not be expensive to retain. Food manufacturers with test kitchens frequently use them.

3. STRUCTURING THE QUESTIONNAIRE.   One of the most difficult tasks in research is constructing a questionnaire that will reveal the truth. The difficulty stems from our personalities: often when people don't know, they would rather lie than admit they don't know. If you've ever been misdirected in a strange town, you know what I mean. Most of us will give ourselves the best of it, in any answer we give. If you ask me how old I am, I'll shave off a couple of years. And if you ask me my income, I'll raise it by a couple of thousand.

Another disconcerting trait is that of telling people what we think they want to hear or what is expected of us. I'm not going to admit I don't care for apple pie with vanilla ice cream on top. *Everybody* is supposed to like apple pie and vanilla ice cream.

Because of these common personality quirks, it is necessary to construct questionnaires in such a way that we do not *ask* the facts, but *allow the respondent to reveal them* For example, if you wished to determine how many people prefer strawberry ice cream, you would not say, "Will those who prefer strawberry ice cream please raise their hands." No, there's too much chance of the kind of distortion mentioned previously. It would be much better to provide the group with a list of six flavors—including strawberry—and ask them to list them in the order of their preference.

4. ANALYZING THE RESULTS.   It is possible to do good research and then ruin the whole project by misinterpreting results. Be careful not to jump to conclusions. Be careful that your own prejudices or preconceived notions don't get in the way. Often the results will indicate something you find hard to believe. Once we did a survey for a chain of stores. The results indicated that customers did not like one particular store. But that store was doing the best business of any in the chain! We began to doubt our results. Further investigation revealed that this store was the only one in town carrying an excellent line of fairly priced merchandise. However, the salespeople had all been with the store for years and waited on customers as though they were doing the customers a favor. Certainly, the customers *didn't* like the store and welcomed the opportunity to tell someone so!

6

The World Will Beat
a Mousetrap
to Your Door

THE MOUSETRAP

A product is not simply an object. Indeed, it represents a complex bundle of benefits and satisfactions that meet a consumer's particular needs and desires.

This concept is a very important one in marketing. In this chapter we are going to be talking about the product, not as a thing, but as a complete package of need-satisfying qualities.

SATISFACTION IS IN THE EYE
OF THE BEHOLDER

Remember that a product is a package of satisfactions. But also keep in mind that for the same product different people see different satisfactions.

Thus, the manufacturer, the reseller, and the consumer may be appealed to by quite different satisfactions in the package. The manufacturer of women's shoes may be delighted by the new design he has achieved. The retailer may be appealed to strongly by the publicity for the new shoe as well as the generous profit margin offered by the manufacturer. The ultimate consumer may have quite different considerations: the satisfaction of being very stylish, the way the shoes make her legs look attractive, or the fun of paying an outrageous price for her first pair of famous designer shoes.

Goods and Services Get Mixed

It is customary to distinguish between companies that make goods and those that provide services. Westinghouse makes goods such as light bulbs and television sets. Orkin provides the service of pest control.

But often your service organization sells goods, and your product manufacturer provides services. Thus IBM, RCA, and other manufacturers of various kinds of equipment have large and active service organizations. The people you call to service your TV also sell parts or goods. You might note also that the place where you buy goods called gasoline and motor oil is often referred to as a service station.

WHY YOU MUST KNOW THE CONTENTS
OF THE PACKAGE

The contents of a product's package of satisfactions is sometimes different or more extensive than you think it is. You must make sure you don't overlook anything.

From reading the ads of the past twenty years, we would be led to believe that motorists buy gasoline at their particular filling stations because that product (a) gives more miles to the gallon, (b) stops engine knock on hills, or (c) provides good motor protection.

I suggest that you now make a survey of your friends. Why do they patronize their present service stations? Because of the reputation of the company, the quality of the product, or the great television commercials? I think you will find they do business there because (a) they can be sure of getting gasoline there during a shortage, (b) the station is convenient, or (c) they like the proprietor and attendants and the way they treat customers.

People buy toothpaste for different reasons: to have a more beautiful smile, to have a fresher-tasting mouth, or to prevent cavities. As a marketer, you won't want to overlook any of these satisfactions present in the toothpaste package. Nor will you want to overlook all those brushers who happen to value one over the others. So you will carefully call attention to available satisfactions in your advertising. In fact, you quite possibly might make a separate toothpaste especially designed to meet the needs and desires of each one of those groups.

WOULD YOU WALK A MILE FOR A ROLLS ROYCE?

There are several different ways to break product packages into classifications. In each case it is done on the basis of the values perceived in the package of satisfactions by the customer. These classifications are, as you will see, quite distinct. We can classify product packages as *industrial* or *consumer*. Consumer packages can be classified as *convenience, shopping,* or *specialty* goods. You have already seen that resellers (retail and wholesale middlemen) look upon product satisfactions with a different view than you do. Now let's see how the ultimate consumer regards the classifications above.

Consumer Goods and Industrial Goods

We can make a broad distinction between the things people buy for themselves and the things they buy for their businesses. You understand now, from previous chapters, some of the buying motivations that move the ordinary consumer. Industrial buyers have quite different motivations. They respond to a very different product package of satisfactions. Here are some of them:

1. *Availability.* It is very important to the industrial buyer to have an assured supply. On-time deliveries may be indispensable to company operations. The lack of a certain nut or bolt could bring a whole assembly line to a halt.

2. *Service.* Industrial machinery and equipment is becoming increasingly complicated and specialized. Breakdowns can prove costly. The buyer wants to be sure that part of any package is fast, expert servicing.

3. *Economic requirements.* Many industrial products are subsidiary parts of a larger product—for example, the nuts and bolts that hold a classroom chair and desk together. Their contributory cost of the overall cost must be strictly controlled.

4. *Design specifications.* Many industrial purchases are standard equipment. Others must be specially designed for particular uses. The seller's ability to design becomes very important.

One popular way of classifying consumer goods is by the way people buy them. However, the way we buy things is often influenced by the way we regard things (that is, what we perceive to be contained in the package of satisfactions). Let's see how this works with *convenience goods, shopping goods,* and *specialty goods.*

CONVENIENCE GOODS.   There are a number of things we buy routinely, day after day. Regularly consumed products such as foods and toiletries fall into this category. Though we purchase most of these brands routinely, we do not do so unthinkingly; it is just that our weighing of the satisfactions has already occurred. We are loyal to these brands. It would take a real effort to convince us to switch from Crest or Post's Raisin Bran or Budweiser beer. Convenience stores flourish on the principle of being able to meet people's needs quickly and conveniently. If you run out of milk for breakfast tomorrow, you are not going to be too particular about whose brand you pick up.

SHOPPING GOODS.   Shopping goods are things we shop for. We spend much more time and effort in examining and comparing the package of satisfactions. Most families give considerable time to the purchase of a new TV set, a refrigerator, or a car. When buying a suit of clothes or a car, you are apt to do some comparison shopping and carefully weigh the satisfactions offered to you. A number of them are liable to come into play: price, style and appearance, uniqueness, reputation of the maker—to say nothing of the whole complex of your personal, social, and psychological needs.

SPECIALTY GOODS.   These are the products we will go to some trouble to obtain. Or, they may be the type or brand we insist on having. There are people who can't be happy unless they are wearing a certain make of necktie or shoe. But they may have to wait until their next trip to Chicago or New York before they can get what they insist on.
    While prices for specialty goods tend to be high, price often is unimportant in the package of satisfactions. In fact, low-priced shopping goods or convenience goods frequently become specialty goods because of the special satisfactions the consumer sees in and derives from this particular package.
    There are people who would not only rather fight than switch; they'd rather go without their dessert than change their beloved brand. They, or someone, have woven a very strong psychological net around themselves to create this fierce loyalty. It's *my* beer, *my* luggage, *my* tailor—and no other.

Later, when we get into advertising and promotion, you will see how advertisers often create these subtle satisfactions to which customers cling. After all, how much difference is there between cola drinks or gasolines?

A PRODUCT'S LIFE IS NOT A BOWL OF CHERRIES

A product package has a life of its own. Just as in our lives, there are certain periods or phases that can be observed in a product's *life cycle*.

Humans have a predictable life span. Our periods of childhood, youth, middle age, and old age are easily identified. There are many definite characteristics connected with our lives at each one of these stages: the growing pains of youth, the ambition and striving of young adulthood, the settled life of middle age, and the quiet, slower retirement years.

Yet there is one big, important difference with products and it is at the heart of marketing problems. Although the phases of a product's life cycle are predictable, the *length* of those phases is not. Will our product have the career of certain rock stars—quickly rising to dizzying heights and then disappearing into obscurity? Or, like Bing or Frank, will it grab and hold the public's acclaim year after year? Much of what is said in this book is about how we can induce our product to grow quickly into a healthy, flourishing youth and how we can help it to enjoy a long, happy, and prosperous middle age.

Let's look at these phases of the product's life cycle.

THE INTRODUCTORY PERIOD.   You have perfected your product and now, with high hopes, you have introduced it into the market.

At this stage, you support the product with as much promotion and advertising as you can afford. You strive to fill the distribution pipeline and to get all possible retail cooperation. If you have a unique product with an outstanding satisfaction appeal, you may set your prices at the *skimming* level (high margins, small portion of market). Certainly your market researchers will be measuring the rate of *repeat purchases;* based on this information, you may make pricing or other changes.

THE STAGE OF MARKET GROWTH.   If your product catches on, you now enter the phase of market growth. The geographical marketing mix may be expanded and new middlemen enlisted to sell your product. The success of the product will have been noticed by your competitors, and you can be sure they will soon be in the market with products similar to yours. Volume production may allow you to cut prices due to reduced costs. Your advertising and promotion should remain intensive.

THE STAGE OF PRODUCT MATURITY. Just as many of us noticed that it was harder to reach our shoelaces after thirty, so a slowing down in the rate of sales increases heralds the product's middle age. Competition will still be stiff, but before long several companies will settle down into fairly stable market positions. It may get more difficult to get and hold good middlemen, particularly if you have won only a marginal share of the market.

This stage of the product's life can last for many years. Innovations may not be serious or unique enough to affect it, and steady improvements may keep it attractive. Products like Coca Cola, Listerine Antiseptic, and Beechnut Chewing Tobacco continue year after year with scarcely a change in product or packaging. But for most products, new features, designs, and improvements are essential to a long phase of maturity.

THE PERIOD OF DECLINE. Here time and competition take their toll. But before withdrawing the product from the market, you milk it for all it is worth. Profit margins are reduced, distribution is cut to outlets still showing significant volume, and advertising and promotion will be drastically reduced. You are not longer as concerned with market share as you once were. You will observe that the same thing is occurring with your competitors.

WHAT'S MY LINE?

Companies have lines of products. Ford produces a line of cars—from Pinto to Lincoln Continental. Major distillers such as Seagrams or National market many different brands under their name. The makers of the Water-Pik have other newer products in their product family.

When we superimpose several life cycles in succession on one another, the peaks and valleys of growth and decline are eliminated. A nice, steady average return on company investment is maintained as fresh players are sent into the game as the old ones tire. This demonstrates just one of the reasons why it is advisable to develop a company line of products.

Note the difference between a *product line* and a *product mix*. The product line is related items with similar manufacturing and marketing problems. A product mix is the total offering of a company and may include quite diverse items. This is particularly true in the day of burgeoning conglomerates. R.J. Reynolds, known for years as the maker of Camel and Winston cigarettes, is today in the candy and consumer food businesses, too.

The sequence of introduction, growth, maturity, and decline in a product's life cycle can be greatly affected by a phenomenon known as the *consumer adoption process*. This is a five-step process that bears some resemblances to the well-known anatomy of a sale: attention, interest, desire, conviction, and decision to buy.

In the *adoption process* the consumer is said to go through five steps: awareness, interest, evaluation, trial, and adoption. This, in effect, is what most of us do in making a purchase decision. What is important is the speed with which this adoption process takes place after you have put a new or innovative product on the market.

On a smaller scale, this happens when you adopt a restaurant. You become aware you are hungry, you think about lunch, you evaluate where you might go, you try out a number of places, and finally settle on one favorite restaurant. Most of the familiar brands and labels that appear in your home week after week have been adopted.

R&D—RESEARCH AND DEVELOPMENT OR RELAX AND DIE

As discussed before, it is vitally important for a company to have a line of products on which it can expend its marketing efforts. Moreover, products must be cared for and improved if the profitable mature phase is to be stretched out. Some products such as automobiles need and receive constant changes. Others, such as Pepsi Cola or Hershey Chocolate Bars haven't changed much over the years.

Yet whether it is a slight change in packaging or a dramatic introduction of a new product, change must take place. New blood must be pumped into the product line if the company is to continue to grow and prosper. Following is the process by which this comes about.

What Is a New Product?

Before we examine this process, let's define exactly what is meant by a new product. Just as a product is more than a thing, so, it turns out, a new product is a lot of different things to a lot of different people.

When you see "NEW!" emblazoned in the headlines of an ad it doesn't always mean *new*. It could mean a new package, a new feature, a new size, a new use, or a new price. Or it *could* mean a product so new and different that it utterly astonishes and delights everyone.

For example, hula hoops, instant cameras, and frozen vegetables burst on the scene as radically new products. While people had long been riding waves and diving under them and skimming over them (particularly in the South Pacific), scuba gear and snorkles, surf boards, and catamarans are new products to most of us.

There is nothing new about soup or coffee. But there *is* something new about instant soups or coffees. Indeed, there is something new about a coffee without the caffeine in it. Arm and Hammer Baking Soda was for a long time something used for baking and indigestion relief. Then it became a new product, one that helped eliminate odors in refrigerators.

Therefore, a new products department or a research and development committee does considerably more than simply create new products.

GETTING READY FOR THE NEW BABY

The constant growing-maturing-declining process happens to different products in the line at different times, not all together. The demand for new products places great responsibility on marketing managers. At the start, there are three places he must look for the right answers. The first is his own company.

DOES THE PRODUCT SUIT THE COMPANY?   Is it the kind of product they logically would be expected to produce? Is it something with which they already have some expertise or at least familiarity?

WHAT ABOUT COSTS?   Is there a reasonable expectation of producing it within reasonable cost limits? Is it the kind of product the company can make without a tremendous investment in new machinery or facilities?

THE DISTRIBUTION CHAIN.   Most manufacturers have spent considerable time and money cementing their relationships with their middlemen and retailers. Will the product fit into the current distribution set-up? Or will it require the cultivation of entirely new and perhaps unfamiliar lines of distribution? Moreover, is this product likely to prove attractive to the middlemen? Will its sales and profit potential prove exciting to them? What kind of shipping and warehousing problems does it present?

THE CONSUMER.   Is there a potential market for this product? What does that market look like right down to the last mole and wrinkle? Does this product have the capability to satisfy any basic social or psychological need or desire?

If marketing managers could get all these answers right and make their decisions with split-second timing, they'd be the happiest people in the world. They can't. The case history books are full of horror stories about companies that didn't get all the answers or misinterpreted the ones they got.

This makes our next subject so important: the creation of new products. Beware. We are now entering the area of ideas. And ideas are very fragile, delicate, and shy. (There is a famous law called Norris's Third Law that says, "Never laugh at anyone with a crazy idea.")

"NEVER LAUGH AT ANYONE WITH A CRAZY IDEA"

New product ideas can come from anywhere. Everyone who handles a product—factory worker, salesperson, wholesaler, retailer, consumer— is capable of coming up with an idea that will improve the present product or create a completely new one. Often, great marketing successes get their start from something as simple as someone saying, "Gee, there must be a better way than this . . ." or, "Why don't we try it *this* way?"

However, most manufacturers prefer not to rely entirely on chance or inspiration. They use a more formal means of making sure they'll get a steady, dependable flow of new product suggestions.

This is done by forming groups or committees with names such as *venture teams* or *new product departments*. In companies with a corporate set-up that includes *brand managers*, these people are often given the responsibility for developing new products.

One interesting way to get improvement or new product ideas was nicknamed brainstorming by Madison Avenue where it originated. Looking for new campaign ideas, a famous adman named Alex Osborn (the "O" in BBD&O) gathered a group of people in a room, giving them some simple ground rules and letting them bounce ideas off one another. The mutual stimulus usually works quite well. Today, this method has been formalized into a recognized technique for generating ideas.

Whichever way they go about it, the people who are responsible for new product ideas have an awesome task. The mortality tables show that the death rate for new product ideas on their way to becoming new products is a frightening and costly one. It has been estimated that the failing rate in the food industry may be as high as 80%.[1] So you see, even the best and biggest of the marketers can't expect to win all the time. The length of time it takes to bring out a new product and get it to market may vary widely, too. Adler has shown that freeze-dried instant coffee took ten years, filter cigarettes took six years, and zippers thirty.[2]

WHO KILLED COCK ROBIN?

New product failures can be traced to a variety of causes. Speaking very generally of the new product failures, it seems to boil down to the fact that marketers didn't find out all the things they should have about their products. Of course, there are several reasons why this could happen. They could be blind, dumb, or too full of wishful thinking. One thing you can be sure of: when your market and product research plays you false, when someone thinks it is saying one thing when it is really saying another, then you are in real trouble.

Product Development and Modification

There are a number of identifiable steps a product passes through on its way to its actual appearance on the market. These are: the generation of the idea itself, from whatever source; the screening of the ideas for practicality and ultimate profitability (the latter screening is often referred to as "business analysis"); the development of the prototype product; the testing of this model; and the ultimate introduction on the market (commercialization).

It has been estimated[3] that about 60% of the time devoted to the development of new product ideas goes into the development and testing areas of product development. The absolute necessity for sound research and correct interpretation of information is never more dramatically shown than in the development and testing areas. Edsel and Frost 8/80 are not alone in Boot Hill Product Cemetery. They have some very distinguished company.

[1] Lee Adler, "Time Lag in New Product Development," Journal of Marketing, Jan. 1966, pp. 17–21.

[2] See T.L. Angelus, "Why Do Most New Products Fail?" Advertising Age, Mar. 24, 1969, p. 85. Other studies by Marketing Communication Research Center, Princeton, N.J., suggest a lower general product rate.

[3] This much-quoted figure is from a study done by Booz, Allen, and Hamilton, New York, in 1968. B.A. and H. is an outstanding firm of business and marketing consultants.

7

How to Carry a Loaf of French Bread

WHAT IT COMES IN IS AS IMPORTANT AS WHAT IT IS

If you look at your bathroom shelves or at the cabinets in your kitchen, you will see what this chapter is all about—packages.

In your home there are packages of all shapes, sizes, and descriptions. Some are made of materials you have never heard of and couldn't pronounce if you had. In terms of packaging sophistication, the modern supermarket is light years ahead of the old general store with its crackers in barrels and its milk in 20-gallon metal cans. And yet the lapse in time is relatively short between general store and supermarket.

The science of packaging has taken a quantum leap in the last generation. The storekeeper of 25 years ago would be astonished at the way his products come to him today. In fact, some marketing people seem a little astonished. There are still many college textbooks that don't admit that packaging is a legitimate part of the marketing mix.

Yet, it is. It also plays a very important part in promotion, as you are going to see.

To put it another way, the way you package your product can't be left to chance or to amateurs. It must receive as serious consideration as any other part of your marketing effort, whether product, price, promotion, or distribution.

FRENCH BREAD.   The Europeans, as you have noticed if you have eaten in one of their restaurants or shopped in one of their stores, are good at packaging, particularly the small ones such as individual pats of butter or servings of jam.

On the other hand, the French have shown us how to get along without packaging, particularly in the food field. The chain store supermarket is unknown in most smaller French towns. Shopping is done at small *patisseries, charcuteries,* and other stores, and packaging can be as simple as a page from this morning's newspaper.

We usually think of French bread as the elongated type although it comes in many shapes. Very often this fresh loaf is carried unwrapped, either under the arm or lengthwise between the handles of a pocketbook. And who is to argue that the golden crust of a loaf of freshly baked French bread is not the most beautiful packaging anyone could conceive?

WHAT PACKAGES ARE MADE OF.   Traditional packaging was mostly paper, glass, tin, or wood. A great deal of it still is. We have paper bags, glass pickle jars, tins of sardines, and boxes of wine bottles.

What has happened in the packaging revolution is that it has proceeded in several different directions. For one thing, though the traditional packaging materials are still around in great quantity, their designs and the way they are being used has changed radically. For example, think of the way a book is sent through the mails in a paper container. The simplest is a book wrapped in heavy paper and secured with adhesive strips. But there are dozens of other paper shipping containers for books. Some are cleverly designed stiff cardboard boxes with patented opening devices, others are soft two-layered padded paper containers. And the new designs never stop.

You may think the Coca Cola bottle has remained unchanged, but it hasn't. The changes have been gradual, but they have been constant. Think of all the different sizes of bottles there are today. A beer bottle used to be long necked and usually it was made of brown glass. It contained 12 fluid ounces. Today you can buy beer in everything from chug-a-lugs to party kegs. And whatever became of the "growler"—the tin bucket filled by the bartender for home consumption?

The art of shaping metals and glass has enabled packagers to do much with traditional materials, too. Look at the shelves of your liquor store during the holidays and you'll see some pretty fancy work, both in glass and paperboard. Cans are no longer cans; they come in an almost unlimited variety of shapes and sizes.

Closures are what packagers call the top or stopper. Here, too, package designers have done some remarkable things. In years past, almost all closures were metal screw caps or corks. Some closures of bottles containing liquids under pressure had caps which were stamped on mechanically. Thus beer and soft drink bottle caps had to be pried open with a bottle-opener.

A whole book could be written about can openers. Cans preserving meat first were used in the Crimean War and were widely in use in the Civil War. The trouble with the cans was there were no can openers—the troops used bayonets and hatchets to open the cans! But inventors have been making up for it ever since. Each year there is a new model. If you look in the back of your kitchen drawer you may find an antiquated lethal little instrument that you pried around the top, creating jagged edges. Today you can buy an electrically-driven beauty that will open the can, remove the top on a magnetic arm, hand it to you, and whistle "Dixie."

THE PLASTIC AGE.   The big jump in packaging technique began after World War II. Although plastics were used at an earlier date, chemists began to make all kinds of synthetic products about that time, stuff that could be extruded in threads or rolled out in sheets and was great for making all kinds of packages.

Of course, chemical companies and designers were quick to point out the advantages of these new plastics, one of the most important being the savings in shipping weight as compared to glass and metal containers. Plastics can also be printed on in color.

In recent years, plastics have led all sectors of the packaging industry's growth and it is anticipated that it will continue to do so. More and more products are being subjected to in-plant packaging; these involve shrink and stretch systems. Another interesting use is the retort or cook-in-the-pouch which preserves food without preparation. The rapid growth of microwave ovens has also stimulated the demand for coated paperboard trays that can resist temperatures up to 425°.

COMBINATIONS.   It is interesting to see how today's package manufacturers and designers use the great number of new materials available to them in addition to the old standbys. Look on the shelves of your supermarket, and you can see for yourself how this has been done.

Plastic closures for all types of glass and plastic containers have become very popular. Some of them are quite cleverly designed. Many plastic half-gallon milk containers have a closure with a ring that makes it possible to remove the cap without spilling milk on the first opening. The development of linerless, leak-proof threaded closures has encouraged the use of plastic caps with a variety of containers.

Processed meats and meat spreads now come in containers which are a combination of coated paperboard and transparent plastic sheet. Grated cheese, flour, and condiment containers are often a combination of metal framing, coated cardboard, and a plastic cover with a movable section that closes the shaker holes.

Most cereals come in cardboard boxes with inside containers of waterproof or metalicized paper. Tins of coffee have plastic tops for use after the metal top has been cut off. Nor should we forget the stoneware jars and bottles that are one of the oldest forms of packaging. (The Greeks shipped oil in jars made of stoneware.) The present jars are given a variety of closures—including wax!

One of the most interesting combinations—used primarily in industry—is foam-in-place packaging in which a liquid foam is sprayed into a package containing shock-sensitive parts or instruments. And, of course, we are all familiar with the packaging industry's response to the need for child-proof safety closures.

HOW TO MAKE A PACKAGE WORK OVERTIME FOR YOU.   Packaging's primary job is to deliver products in an unspoiled and uncontaminated condition. This is a job it does admirably. New methods of sealing and binding sometimes make it difficult for even the customer to get at the product. The strength of plastics and these new sealing methods have made it possible to pack many products under pressure and even to inject preservative gases as in some sandwich meat packaging.

Aside from enabling us to move products from place to place without injury or contamination, packaging carries out some other marketing functions that can be extremely important.

PACKAGING AS A DISPLAY PIECE.   Packages make displays; it's as simple as that. And groups of packages make big displays. To put it another way, a package acts as a display piece and it is best to keep this in mind.

If your package is a retail item, it is going to be on the shelf with many other products. Which one is going to catch the eye—and interest—of the consumer?

In the retail food field, salespeople fight fiercely for shelf space and shelf position. They know that the number of linear feet and the nearness to eye level are going to play a large part in the movement of their products. Something the salesperson can't do anything about, but *you* can, is how attractive a picture your products make en masse. When you work with your package designer, it is essential to keep this in mind.

A stroll through a supermarket or chain drugstore will demonstrate this to you. Remember: A customer only sees a package individually *after* it has been purchased and brought home.

One of the cleverest uses of packaging for display was for brooms. The manufacturer encased the business end of the broom in a plastic bag with colorful design and printing. When a dozen brooms were placed upright in a container, it made a very striking display—something like a big bunch of roses towering over the counter.

Shipping containers themselves are a very practical form of display. Look at any checkout counter in your store. Small items such as gum, candy, and tobacco products usually come to the retailer packed in one-dozen units. When the top is raised and fixed in position, this unit becomes a self-contained display unit.

This works for larger shipping cases, too. These are referred to as cut cases. The retailer cuts open the shipping carton along certain lines, folds back the pieces, and then has a nice floor display.

FIGURE 1. Cut cases often carry instructions for the dealers; this is a relatively simple one.

THE PACKAGE AS A PROMOTION.   One of the best ways to make a package work for you is to use it as a vehicle for a merchandising promotion. There are many ways this can be handled; let's look at a few.

The food shopping ads in Thursday's paper contain dozens of cents-off coupons. Another place to put that coupon is on the package itself. This coupon may entitle the purchaser to a discount on the packaged item, or for another item in the company's product line.

Premiums are often placed inside the package with the outside of the package used to announce the premium. Thus, a package may say: "FREE INSIDE, ATTRACTIVE DISH TOWEL."

The back panel of breakfast cereal packages is often used to promote the self-liquidating premium. A self-liquidating premium is one that pays for itself. For example, for only $2.00 plus the tops of two cartons as proofs-of-purchase, I may offer to send your youngster a baseball autographed by the National or American League baseball team of his or her choice. The $2.00 plus the profit from the two packages should cover the cost of the whole deal.

Two-fers are when two packages are attached together by the manufacturer (for example, a razor and razor blades or a toothbrush and toothpaste) and the customers receive two items for the price of one.

Mini-packaging, the packaging of very small items such as an individual portion of catsup or two aspirin tablets, is ideal for the sampling promotional device. Sometimes a physician gives patients needed medicine rather than writing out a prescription for it. These are usually specially packaged samples of the medication that have been left with him by the pharmaceutical company's detail man.

THE PACKAGE AS SALESPERSON.   The easier it is for you to use a product and the more successfully it performs for you, the more likely you are to use it. The package can help this come about.

For one thing, the manufacturer doesn't want you to misuse the product and be disappointed in the results. Thus, in all but the most obvious cases, your package is likely to carry "Directions For Use." For example, a package of soap powder for dishwashers warns that the water must be hot (140°), that dishes must be placed so that soiled surfaces face the water spray, and that all the detergent cups in the washer are filled. The package even goes on with advice on how to solve common dishwashing problems and how to care for silver.

Some products have information on use inside the package itself. Others contain leaflets and brochures that are practically a short course on how to finish furniture or how to adjust a camera or how to use a flash attachment.

There are packages that are such good salespersons, they call out to you from the shelf. They are not satisfied with just being seen. They want to be heard. Sunsweet Prunes reminds you that they are "The smart snack," presumably for dieters. Cascade dishwashing detergent says it is "For virtually spotless dishes." Nestle's Souptime reminds you that it is the "10 second soup" and Betty Crocker Gingerbread cries out to you, "Treat your family to something special."

Packages can talk to you in pictures, too. Food packages are ideal for this, showing people enjoying the product or a picture of the product itself. Mueller's rigatoni has a plastic window in the package that lets you look at the product itself.

THE PACKAGE AS A CONSUMER SERVICE.   There are two other aids to the consumer that come with almost every package. One of these is a specific set of facts regarding the contents of the package—what it contains and how much. Almost all packaged foods devote a panel to nutrition information such as calories, proteins, carbohydrates, and percentages of the daily recommended allowance of vitamins, calcium, and iron. There is also, usually on the same panel, a list of all product ingredients. This list includes water, preservatives, flavorings, and everything else that has gone into the product. Most of this is covered by laws enforced by the Federal Trade Commission.

When products can be dangerous to skin or eyes or poisonous if swallowed, the packages must display a prominent danger notice, often including the antidote. Exact net weights have eliminated much of the price confusion resulting from economy size and giant economy size.

THE PACKAGE AS SUGGESTION-MAKER.   As you know, one of the best ways to increase sales volume is to increase product usage. When I was a kid, many adolescents ate yeast cakes to clear up their complexion problems. (This wasn't just a fad, the medical profession believed it, too.) Millions of yeast cakes were sold, not for raising dough, but for eliminating skin blemishes.

The recipes on many food packages are attempts to multiply use and thereby increase sales volume.

While recipes show the homemaker ways to more quickly consume the product, food packaging is not alone in using this increased use device. Almost any package can carry it. A 1-oz. can of 3-In-One Household Oil carries illustrations of a sewing machine, hinge, and electric tool. The copy reminds us this is, "The finest oil for hinges, hand tools, garden tools, toys and appliances . . . anywhere a light lubricant is needed."

The lesson is clear: Whenever you put anything in a package, let the package suggest as many ways as possible the product can be used.

BRANDING ISN'T JUST FOR COWS.   Labels, brand names, and trademarks are all a part of the package. Often, as in the case of Campbell Soup, the label is to all intents the package. The label and various parts of the package are your calling card, and it will pay you to give them your utmost attention and care.

A line of products may have a brand name, such as Betty Crocker baking products or Green Giant vegetables. Other companies have brands with individual names and distinctive label designs. For example, J.W. Dant Bourbon Whiskey is a National Distillers brand, although one would not be able to tell this from the label. Note that Betty Crocker and Green Giant are also trademarks. The scripted name "Coca Cola" is also a trademark.

A character may be part of your label or your trademark. Cream of Wheat has a Chef and Aunt Jemima is portrayed on pancake flour packages. How about Aldo, that exuberant character who walks through the Cella commercials?

Trademarks, whether they are names, characters, or designs, should be registered for exclusive use and must be searched (that is, determination must be made as to whether anyone has already registered it). Companies are sometimes driven to court when a competitor picks a name that is almost theirs. This happened to Listerine Antiseptic and Phillips Petroleum Company. In the case of Listerine, the competitor imitated the entire labeling and package.

BATTLING BRANDS.   There is war between nationally advertised brands and private label brands created by stores themselves. Private labels are created by stores that want to have a line somewhat lower in price than the nationally advertised brands. That is, they want to be able to satisfy the cost-conscious or bargain-hunting customer.

Many chain food stores have canners pack fruits and vegetables with their own labels on the cans. They sell these for 20% to 30% less than the nationally advertised brands. Sears, as another example, has stoves and refrigerators with Sears' own trade name on them, Kenmore. The stoves and refrigerators were made for Sears by a U.S. manufacturer.

You can see the problem. A retailer of General Electric or Westinghouse refrigerators hates to see practically the same item being sold at lower prices under another name, taking business away from him. Retailers let the manufacturer know exactly how they feel. Also, food processors who have spent millions promoting their products and sending people into the retail stores don't appreciate seeing the customer switched away to a lower-cost unadvertised brand.

LEONARDO IN A BROOKS BROTHERS' SHIRT—THE PACKAGE DESIGNER

It seems there are many people who don't take package designers or package design very seriously. They seem to think that packages just happen, as an afterthought. But it is one of marketing's most important activities; a wrong choice can kill you. It will be well worth your while to look through a publication such as *Modern Packaging* and see the kind of beauty and ingenuity that is being displayed here and in Europe today.

Big manufacturers and their advertising agencies leave no stone unturned in their efforts to attain outstanding packaging. Design may be done by a studio specializing in package design or by the agency's art department.

What can you—as a non-corporate giant—do to help assure yourself of a good package design? Here are a few suggestions:

DECIDE WHAT YOU WANT YOUR PACKAGE TO DO FOR YOU.   This can cover a lot of ground, but consider this: You may not want the most strikingly beautiful package possible. In fact, it may be to your advantage to have a package that is plain, unassuming, and seems to say, "What's inside is a good, honest product."

WHAT KIND OF PEOPLE ARE YOU TRYING TO ATTRACT?   Kellogg's Nutri-Grain package is a daring departure from other Kellogg cereal packages—or from anyone's cereal package now on the shelf. There is a great deal of white space. The drawings of raisins and grains are textbook-like. The predominant color of the printed copy is purple with yellow grain and the words "no sugar added" in light blue. The effect is far different from that of most cereal boxes. There are no premium offers on the other panels but, in effect, lectures on the benefits of whole grain.

Kellogg is not aiming at the usual market for cereals. It is after a new market segment: the growing number of natural-foods-and-nutrition-conscious people who know a lot about whole grain, germs, and fibers.

HOW MUCH SHOULD YOUR PACKAGE COST?   The ratio between product cost and package cost can vary tremendously. Sometimes, as in perfumes and gift liquor packages, the high packaging cost can be justified. But frequently, simple packaging is the best. Don't overspend, even though the package may be beautiful.

IS A NEW KIND OF PACKAGING JUSTIFIED?   The L'Eggs egg-shaped package departed completely from traditional hosiery packaging. It was tied in to the whole new marketing concept. Listerine Antiseptic, on the other hand, wouldn't dream of changing its package, unattractive though it may be.

ART STUDIOS.   Unless you are fortunate enough to have an advertising agency with a big and talented art department—and few businesses are—you will be wise to take your packaging design problems to an art service or studio. Work closely with the artist and make sure he knows all about your product, your market segment, and your competition.

There is another possibility; the printer of your label or the manufacturer of your package may be able to supply art and design help. Look through the trade magazines. They list many of the most brilliant designers. Or do what was recommended before; call the editors of Packaging Design or Packaging Engineering and ask for help. They'll be more than helpful.

8

The Price Is Right

PRICE TAGS ARE A MERCHANT'S BEST FRIEND

In the old days, the life of the average Persian rug salesman was not all pomegranates and kurds. As you would have discovered as a salesman, there were many factors that determined the price you charged for your merchandise other than your well-earned reputation as a haggler.

For one thing, the date harvest may have been poor that year and everyone was holding onto his money. The caravan from Baluchistan was late due to a new Bedouin leader who raised the price of safe conduct through his territory. Ali-ben-Rancid, operating out of the Street of Thieves, cut prices again. You and your rug-selling friends were sitting around the coffeehouse trying to think up ways to discourage him without calling too much attention on yourselves by the Grand Vizier. You were thinking of installing a less costly line of rugs. However, since the country had been at peace for the past year, overproduction might drive prices down. You feared getting stuck with a costly inventory.

Any modern marketing director will tell you that some things are different. For example, it is no longer necessary to cry real tears while informing the prospective buyer that, in letting your product go at this ridiculous price, you are condemning your entire family to a life of poverty and bondage.

Otherwise, things haven't changed very much in pricing since the Persian rug salesman's day. The modern marketing manager has all the problems the ancient had plus a few modern wrinkles the vendor of rugs never dreamed of. Let's look at some of them.

KNOW THYSELF

WHAT KIND OF COMPANY ARE YOU?   When it comes to figuring out how much you want to get for what you sell, there are several broad considerations. One of the important ones is the reputation of your company. How do you look to the public? What do they think of when they see your name or your trademark? For instance, if you have been making high-quality watches that you have been selling for relatively high prices for years, you would not suddenly introduce a watch made and priced for the mass market. At least, you'd think very seriously about it because that cheap watch could badly hurt your image as a manufacturer of high-priced, high-quality merchandise.

HOW OLD IS YOUR PRODUCT?   If you have a new product or one that has been on the market for some time that is certainly going to have a lot to do with the price you charge.

If you have a new and excitingly different product, you may be able to charge quite a bit for it. You can anticipate that many people are going to want it simply because it is new and different.

Perhaps you are bringing out a new product and would like to get lots of people to try it. In that case, you might put a very low price on it to encourage buyers.

You might even have an old product whose popularity is beginning to wane. To stimulate sales and keep it popular, you would cut prices.

You may find that sometimes simply lowering the price doesn't result in stimulated sales. It depends on what product you are selling. Some products such as coffee are quite sensitive to price change and will show an immediate demand. With some others such as gasoline, demand seems to stay level whether the price goes up or down.

HOW FAR DOES YOUR PRODUCT HAVE TO BE SHIPPED?   Like the rug seller whose caravan was delayed, you must consider how far your product is going to be shipped. How many people are going to have to handle it for you? Where is it going to be stored and for how long? All these people must make a profit, too. So you will figure this into your price structure.

HOW MUCH DOES IT COST TO MAKE IT?   Of course, you want to know accurately how much it costs for you to manufacture your product. How much do the raw materials cost? How much for the labor? How much for your heat and light and rent? When you get a figure for all that, then you can add on a gross margin of profit out of which may come other things such as shipping charges and advertising allowances.

But wait a minute. Do you want to set your prices high enough so that you make a profit right away? Or are you willing to wait awhile before you begin enjoying your profits? You see, production costs tend to level off or to come down as you increase the quantity of the product you make. And the more you sell, the more profit you make. So, even though you started out losing money, after awhile, if things go as you hope, profits are going to equal the cost of production. This is called the *break-even point*. After that, everything is gravy.

People who sell by mail are very conscious of their break-even point. They know exactly how many coupons or orders they must get back before they recover their initial investment.

WHAT ARE YOUR COMPETITORS DOING?   If you are new to a market or even if you have an old product, the last thing you want is to get involved in a price war. Your competitors are going to be keeping a close watch on you.

There have been cases where a big competitor has driven a small competitor right out of the field by drastically lowering his prices. So you are going to determine the price range for your particular kind of product and stick pretty close to it. You'll be able to tailor your price by adjusting production and other costs.

The nickel candy bar was a standard item of merchandise for a long time. But as manufacturing costs and chocolate costs went up, the profits got slimmer. For as long as they could, candy manufacturers kept their traditional nickel price by making the candy bar smaller. Today a fifteen-cent bar is about as big as a five-cent bar used to be.

WHAT KIND OF CUSTOMERS DO YOU HAVE?   As discussed, merchandise can be separated into convenience, shopping, and specialty products. Price plays a part in the way customers react to different kinds of goods.

Specialty goods, such as famous-name designer clothes, antiques, and paintings, have the kind of customers who attach the least importance to prices. They know what they want and are often willing to pay through the nose to get it. Often the customer will be a little disappointed if the price isn't high. That leaves the seller with a great deal of room for moving prices around.

MAKE SURE YOU KNOW WHAT YOU ARE SHOOTING AT

Different companies have different policies that lead to the goals or objectives they hope to reach through their price practices. Let's look at some of these.

THE TARGET YOU ARE SHOOTING FOR.   Most companies have a profit objective: for roughly how much money they'd like to make on a given product or for their whole line of products. Usually they express this in terms of the return on the money they had to spend to put the product into production and keep it there. They set themselves a fair return and then adjust prices so that the percentage return they need is assured.

KEEPING PRICES ON AN EVEN KEEL.   You may be in a business that is subject to wild swings in prices. Seasonal demand, competition, or other factors may drive prices down or up. Since these wild swings in prices can have unforeseen effects on all your business calculations, you will seek to avoid them wherever possible. Through price advertising and suggested prices, you will do all you can to keep price fluctuations in your trade within manageable limits.

GETTING YOUR PIECE OF THE MARKET.   Earlier we spoke of share of market. A company that produces toothpaste and shaving cream along with several other companies doesn't want to drive everyone else out of the market. But it does expect, through its marketing activities, to get a fair share of that market. That market share is a goal of its policy, and price is one of the things it takes into consideration in working toward that goal.

REACTING TO YOUR COMPETITION.   There are some industries in which the price action of a leading company is almost surely followed by a reaction on the part of the other companies. Let one big steel company, for example, "adjust" its prices and the others almost always play follow-the-leader. It is their policy to maintain their competitive position relative to the other companies.

THIRTEEN WAYS TO MAKE
A PRICE TAG WORK FOR YOU

There are certain common things retailers and manufacturers do in setting their prices. Some make sense. Others may be part of the mythology of retailing.

THOSE ODD PRICES.   I'm sure you have looked at a tag marked "$1.99" and wondered to yourself why they didn't just price it at $2.00 and let it go at that. Though there is little statistical evidence to show its effectiveness, this device is loved by retailers.

LINES OF PRICES.   We mentioned earlier advantages of having a line of products. This makes it possible to have a price for every

FIGURE 2. Liquor store pricing tactics. Note the wide variety in prices and the use of odd pricing.

pocketbook. Sporting goods retailers will have a number of golf club sets on sale. They will range from a low-priced starter set to the costly professional or executive set with a well-known golfer's name on it.

STATUS PRICING.   Some people expect to pay more for the best—and are perfectly willing to do so. Don't forget, too, that paying top dollar for a product shows the world that the buyer always goes first class. Prestige labels on bottles, clothes, and cars can always demand the highest prices.

FIRM PRICE AND NEGOTIABLE PRICE.   Most big manufacturers and retailers put a price on their products and that's it. But there are many cases in which prices can be negotiated, that is, bargained over. It often happens when the buyer has the clout represented by a big order or when the seller is hungry for business. Frequently a price adjustment is negotiated by means of certain allowances: shipping, billing, or advertising.

PRICING FOR SKIMMING AND PENETRATION.   The strategy of *skimming the cream off the market* often occurs when a company is able to introduce a new or unique product which seems to be assured of a strong initial demand. The Polaroid camera or the pocket calculator are examples of this kind of product. Anticipating a limited time to enjoy uniqueness or exclusivity, the manufacturer puts a high price on the product. The manufacturer obliges those who must have one or be the first to have one at a premium.

Penetration pricing occurs at the other end of the scale. A new product or a new firm, entering the market for the first time, is willing to pay a premium to do so. In order to get a foothold in the market, the manufacturer reduces the price of the product to an attractive level. The company accepts losses or barely breaking even as the price it must pay for the privilege of joining the club.

In both skimming and penetration pricing, the price structure will inevitably change. As new competitors enter the market, the skimmer will be forced out of his high profit position. Once the product with the penetration price has introduced itself and gained an acceptable share of market, its price will be brought into line with levels prevailing in the industry.

PRICE DISCOUNTING.   Manufacturers, middlemen, and retailers often offer their customers a break on the listed price in return for certain actions on the buyer's part.

Quantity discounts are a way of saying, "Thank you for the big order." A company will publish a schedule of quantity discounts in which prices are reduced as the size of the order increases. The company may offer this discount schedule on a cumulative basis. In this case, the sum of the buyer's orders within a given time will qualify him for greater discounts.

When a manufacturer distributes through a middleman, he offers a *trade discount*—that is, a discount to the trade for certain services. The middleman then marks up his price when he sells to the retail trade. A manufacturer's trade discount may differ with the customer; the manufacturer must be careful not to create a situation in which a large retail customer is placed in an advantageous position over an important wholesaler of his products through giving both the same trade discount.

Promotional discounts, in which the manufacturer absorbs certain advertising or promotion costs by retailer or wholesaler, are discussed in detail in Chapter 11.

IMPLIED BARGAINS.   A jumble display—goods piled willy-nilly in a basket or shopping cart—is an implied bargain. The implication from the jumbled state of the goods is that they are about to be thrown away and are going at a bargain. The sign over them will say something like "While they last—your choice, any one 89¢."

CENTS-OFF STICKERS.   These can be a sticker or tag or printed right on the carton such as "Special—20% Off."

COUPONS.   These are frequently found in food ads and on or inside cartons. Presentation to the cashier entitles the purchaser to a discount.

FREE GOODS.   "One free with the purchase of a dozen" is, in effect, a price discount. It is popular with wholesalers and retailers alike.

TRADING STAMPS.   The familiar "Green Stamps" appear to be discounting something from the price by giving the customer something of value in the form of a redeemable stamp. But note that there is also a little psychological thrust here: people like the idea of being prudent savers.

LOSS LEADERS.   Stores will often put an attractively low price on a popular item (say, coffee) in order to attract customers and build store traffic. Food stores in particular are plagued by "cherry pickers" who travel from store to store, picking up the specials. Thus stores say, "One can to a customer with $5.00 minimum order." Be careful of the bait and switch. An item not in stock is advertised at an attractively low price. The customer who comes in is then switched to a high-profit item. This practice is illegal.

HOW TO GIVE A LITTLE AND GET A LOT

The fact that customers (and competitors) are located at various distances from the seller's shipping point raises problems involving costs of transportation. No company wants to lose a potentially valuable customer because he is located just a little too far away. Therefore, shippers have developed certain practices to meet this situation. Their prices will depend on the practice followed.

Free On Board (commonly abbreviated F.O.B.) means that the buyer assumes the cost of transportation from the seller's loading platform. "F.O.B. Detroit" refers to the cost of the car before it is shipped to the agency's showroom. You may be familiar with cash-and-carry retail or wholesale outlets in your town. This is also F.O.B.

Some manufacturers find it advantageous to build the shipping costs into their quoted price and charge everyone the same. They simply average the costs of all shipping—near and far—and pass this cost on to the buyer. Thus, the price is the same to all customers, regardless of distance. This is usually referred to as delivered or postage stamp pricing.

When a marketer is fighting for business with a competitor who enjoys an advantage due to his proximity to the customer, he will often resort to freight absorption. He will seek to wipe out the competitor's advantage by equalizing; he absorbs the difference between his shipping cost and the competitor's shipping cost, thus bringing his charge in line with the competitor's.

In the case of marketers of particularly heavy or bulky products in which shipping costs play an important part, zone pricing is often used. The seller divides his marketing area into zones in which all buyers pay the same shipping charges. By this means, the blow is softened somewhat and a bad competitive situation avoided.

A VALUABLE TIP FROM
THE MAIL ORDER MARKETERS

B.E.P.—THE BREAK-EVEN POINT. No one watches the magic B.E.P. closer than the mail order or direct mail business. With them the question is not whether business is good or bad; it's where do you stand in relation to your B.E.P. It's a simple calculation and can be applied to any business.

FIGURE 3. Work area of a mail-order letter house. Here machines automatically fill and address envelopes and handle other mailing pieces.

Let's take a firm selling discount golfing equipment through a catalogue. They have two kinds of costs—*fixed* and *variable*. The fixed costs are the daily costs of being in business such as heat, light, wages, and so on. In this case, the variable cost is the cost of producing the catalogue; the more catalogues printed, the higher the cost. Total revenues are the dollars generated by the orders from the catalogues. The B.E.P. occurs when these revenues *just equal* the fixed costs plus the variable costs. From that point on, the firm is making a profit on each new order that comes in.

HOW TO FIND THE MOST PROFITABLE PRICE

As you've heard, there are economic laws about price and supply and demand. Economists point out that price is a function of demand; this is called a "demand curve"—as the price goes down, the demand goes up, and vice versa. And then the economists mutter, "everything else being equal." This is where the economists and the marketers often part ways because, as the marketers say, "Damnit, things never *are* equal!"

But generally speaking when prices go up, demand goes down. If this is so, then it is quite possible that there is one particular price that will generate more revenues than any of the others. See the table for an example.

Price	Units Sold (Demanded)	Revenue
$10.00	600	$6000.00
8.00	800	6400.00
5.00	1000	5000.00

In this theoretical case the price of $8.00 would seem to be best for you. But remember from your B.E.P. that cost is a variable of units made and sold. Therefore, your picture would look like this:

Price	Unit Sales	Revenue	Total Costs	Profits
$10.00	600	$6000.00	$3000.00	3000.00
8.00	800	6400.00	3000.00	3400.00
5.00	1000	5000.00	3400.00	1600.00

Indeed, the $8.00 price *would* be best for you!

MARGINAL COST AND REVENUE.   There is another profit maximization theory you should be aware of. Marginal means the cost or revenues of making or selling one more unit. This theory says that the ideal price–quantity point comes when marginal cost is equal or slightly less than marginal revenue.[1]

RATE OF TURNOVER.   An important factor that must be considered in setting prices is the rate at which the product sells. An important piece of real estate may be held off the market for years awaiting the favorable moment for selling. In a giant food market, shelves must be replenished constantly as customers empty them. This is why food retailers can sometimes point out proudly what a tiny profit they make on a single item.

STAYING WITHIN THE LAW

Pricing and price tactics can bring you in conflict with the law if you are not careful. While it is usually the big boys who get caught up in the

[1] For a complete explanation of profit maximization and marginal cost and revenue with charts and curves see E. Jerome McCarthy, *Basic Marketing*, 7th ed. (Homewood, Ill.: Richard D. Irwin, Inc.), pp. 511–69.

toils of the law—or at least seem to be the ones who make the news—the laws apply to everyone.

The body of the law regarding prices is covered by:

The Sherman Act, having to do with fixing or controlling prices.

The Clayton Act, covering price discrimination by manufacturers.

The Federal Trade Commission Act, covering deception in selling, including deceptive pricing.

The Robinson-Patman Act, which prohibits price discrimination on goods "of like grade and quality."

The Wheeler-Lea Amendment to Robinson-Patman, further covering deception in pricing.

In addition, there are state and local consumer protection laws enforced by consumer protection agencies.

One of the best ways to learn what is going on legally is to look at the legal section of any recent issue of the *Journal of the American Marketing Association.* This section reviews all types of cases brought by the Federal Trade Commission. Cases involving price are covered separately. The F.T.C. wins some and loses some. The judge's determination and opinion are summarized. You'll find it very instructive.

Of course, the best advice of all is still, "When in doubt, see a lawyer!"

EVERYBODY HAS TO MAKE A PROFIT

As you have seen, price can be used in a great many ways to make a profit. But whatever is done, the profit has to be there if people are going to stay in business. The manufacturer, the wholesale distributor, and the retailer all have to make a profit.

A mark-up at retail or wholesale generally refers to the percentage of the cost added on by the reseller. Thus, if a retailer pays $1.00 for an item and sells it for $1.50, his "mark-up" or gross revenue, expressed as a percentage, is 33⅓%.

$$\frac{.50}{1.50} = 33\tfrac{1}{3}\%$$

The wholesaler does much the same thing, though with greater volume his mark-up is traditionally lower and varies with the services offered by the business.

The manufacturer, in turn, has set his sights on the profit margin necessary to him if he is to stay in business and pay his investors a decent return. What we have then is three mark-ups, for the manufacturer, wholesaler, and retailer.

9

Fishybacks, Birdybacks, and the Pony Express

The process of distribution—getting products to the consumer—is one of the great controllable factors in the marketing mix. It has been said that, of all the factors, this one is the most exciting for it is the least understood and still offers the greatest opportunities for change, new efficiencies, and greater savings. Peter Drucker, a highly regarded marketer, has written a book referring to physical distribution as "The Frontier of Modern Management."

Distribution will be covered from two different angles: first, in terms of the *means* and *facilities* in getting the product from manufacturer to consumer; and, in the next chapter, in terms of the *people* and *institutions* that play a part in helping the movement. The first of these is called *physical distribution*, while the second is usually recognized as *channels of distribution*.

There are two important factors for you to keep in mind. First, it is a *continuous* system. It isn't just a matter of getting the products to the retail store; it is a matter of maintaining a continuous flow of goods out and orders in. It is also a system with a great many variables. You will discover that the way in which these variables are juggled can play an important role in your marketing success.

HOW TO CHOOSE A CARRIER

When most of us think of distribution, we think first of the common means of transportation we see every day: ships, trucks, railroads, and delivery vans of various kinds. Let us begin, then, by looking at the way things are carried and by whom (they are generally referred to as carriers).

Railroads

In terms of tonnage, the most important way to transport products is the railroad. There was a time in our history when the railroad was *the* form of transportation. Indeed, it opened the West. Today its most efficient function is the transportation of *bulk commodities*, often for long distances. In the coal-mining states, miles of loaded coal cars roll from mines to distant power plants. In the South, flat cars piled high with pine logs make their way to paper mills. Railroad tank cars carry chemicals and petroleum products. Flat cars with special frames carry automobiles.

There have been great railroads that played an important part in diplomatic relations: the Cape to Cairo, the Berlin to Bagdad, and the Trans-Siberian linking Leningrad to Vladivostok on the Sea of Japan. Nor should we forget the shortlines—tiny but important roads that have all but disappeared. There were such "shorties" as the Bellefonte Central that ran the 18 miles from Bellefonte to State College, Pennsylvania. Some had romantic names such as the Mississippi, Ouachita, and Red River R.R. in Arkansas. Hawaiian sugar plantations maintained their own shortlines with special steam engines built for them by the Baldwin Locomotive Works.

Ships and Barges

Throughout our history, ships and barges have played an important role in the development of the United States. Boston, San Francisco, Seattle, Baltimore, Norfolk, and San Diego are all famous and busy ports. Millions of tons of products carried by clippers, square riggers, ocean freighters, and giant, modern oil tankers have flowed in and out of them.

FIGURE 4. Containers being loaded aboard ship by means of a rail-mounted gantry crane.

The building of the Erie Canal was an event celebrated in song and story. With its barge traffic, it opened up the West to the New York harbor. On our rivers and intracoastal waterways, barges and freighters transport sand, gravel, gasoline, and fuel oil.

Pipelines

Unseen by most of us, pipelines lace the nation, carrying natural gas and petroleum products. Even coal can be shipped by pipeline in the form of slurry—a mixture of fragmented coal and water. Perhaps the best-known, as well as the most controversial, pipeline is the Trans-Alaska Pipeline System (TAPS). It runs from Prudhoe Bay on the Beaufort Sea, north of the Arctic Circle, to its terminus at Valdez on Prince William Sound on the Gulf of Alaska in Pacific waters. Its construction was a monumental task achieved under the most adverse conditions.

Trucks

The tremendous boom in road building in the United States has made motor transportation extremely important. Four-lane highways span the nation and connect our major cities. Truck lines carry goods to warehouses where they are unloaded. New cargoes are then reassembled and shipped to local points. This is called "break-bulk" and "make-bulk." While all kinds of goods are shipped by truck, more packaged items than bulk items are carried.

Air

Though there was some commercial transportation by plane before World War II, it was after the war that air freight transportation came into its own. Today, there is a freight-forwarding office at every major air terminal. Air freight, of course, has limitations as to size and type of cargo. But some wonderful things have been carried by air, including a hippopotamus from Africa bound for a United States zoo and a racing car bound for the Daytona 500.

Others

There are a number of other ways of shipping with which you may be familiar. United Parcel Service picks up and guarantees delivery within three days. Greyhound and other bus lines transport small packages. The U.S. Postal Service, although beset with problems, is also a popular carrier of small packages, particularly during the holidays. Freight forwarders are in the business of consolidating shipments in order to save shippers money. LCL (less than carload lots) and LTL (less than truckload lots) are familiar phrases to transportation people. The LCL or LTL rate-per-ton is higher than the full load rate. Hence, there are savings in consolidation.

FIGURING OUT THE
TRANSPORTATION PAY-OFF

One reason why distribution is a new frontier is the number of variables involved. Here are some you have to think about: Air is very fast and adheres to schedule very well, but it is expensive. Waterborne transportation is inexpensive, but it is also slow and delivery dates are uncertain. Trucks are costly, but they are faster than everything but air and are quite reliable in meeting delivery dates. Rail falls about in the middle as to cost and speed, but has a high rate of loss due to damage and pilferage.

The Regulation of Carriers

The carriers in the various forms of transportation are regulated by federal and state agencies. The Interstate Commerce Commission regulates railroads, motor carriers, and domestic water carriers. The Civil Aeronautics Board regulates carriers of commercial air freight. The Federal Maritime Board is the controlling body over international waterborne carriers. In addition, carriers operating within state lines are subject to the regulations of certain state bodies.

These regulatory bodies recognize four different forms of transportation. Let's examine each of these.

COMMON CARRIERS.   Railroads, pipelines and interstate truck lines are common carriers whose rates and routes are strictly controlled by the I.C.C. Rates and service charges must be approved by the regulatory body and published.

CONTRACT CARRIERS.   These are carriers owning equipment (such as flat-bed trucks) who contract with concerns to do hauling. Their rates are published, but they are free to make any deal they wish with their customers. Their permits usually cover the type of commodity to be carried and the routes over which they will operate.

EXEMPT CARRIAGE.   These are haulers who carry unprocessed products to market, operate in restricted areas, or are ships or barges carrying three or less commodities in bulk. Their exemption is limited to charges but not to safety standards. A sand barge or fishing boat would fall in this category.

PRIVATE TRANSPORTATION.   These are businesses that, as a part of conducting business, operate their own transport. Bottlers operate their own delivery trucks. Chain stores have their own trucks that move merchandise from warehouse to retail store. As company-owned and operated transport, they are not subject to regulation.

Coordinated Systems

An interesting growing trend in physical transportation is the coordination of the common carriers—trucks, ships, planes, and railroads. These combinations have some interesting names.

Fishyback—truck, ship.
Piggyback—truck, train.
Birdyback—truck, plane.
Rail-water—freight cars, ship.

Containerization

One of the most significant developments in the past few years is the increased use of specially designed shipping containers. These boxes are especially fitted for handling by giant gantry cranes. They come in three sizes—20 ft., 30 ft., and 40 ft. lengths. Weight capacity is generally 40,000 lbs. Packing freight in locked unit containers speeds handling and cuts down on damage and pilferage. Today, it is estimated that containers arriving at ports via trucks and trains account for 35% of ship's cargo. *Freight bulk* is uncontainerized merchandise such as automobiles, tractors, steel beams, and other merchandise which cannot be boxed.

FIGURE 5. A fork lift is being used to unload coffee bags on pallets from a container.

HOW HIGH CAN YOU PILE IT— AND WHERE?

Trucks and planes and freight trains are all around us. But there is another side of transportation that is not quite so obvious. Transported merchandise, tons of which are carried and delivered in various ways, must be stored for redistribution.

Warehouses and Distribution Points

When a refrigerator truck arrives from the West with a cargo of beef carcasses destined for a food chain, its cargo is unloaded and held in the chain store's main refrigerated warehouse. In the cases of beef, which is improved by aging, or bananas which arrive from Central America green, they are warehoused. But the warehouse becomes a distribution center when the beef carcasses are butchered into more manageable sizes and trucked to the chain's various stores where the steaks and chops and hamburger will eventually be sold.

Storage warehousing is regarded as a storing and holding operation. Distribution warehousing is regarded as a gathering and redis-

FIGURE 6. Storage warehouse with coffee bags on pallets.

tributing operation. As in the cases of beef and bananas, it is possible for both functions to take place on the same premises. In fact, this is the usual procedure in a wide variety of businesses. Bulk products, however, are usually held for longer periods of time. Wheat, for instance, is harvested and arrives on the market during certain months. It must be held in grain elevators (a form of warehouse) until demand gradually reduces it. *Tank farms* around every city hold many barrels of gasoline or fuel oil for redistribution to retailers.

Trucks often carry merchandise to a warehouse to be reshipped. These are known as *break-bulk* warehouses. Sears Roebuck has a system of warehouses throughout the country where goods in bulk are received, broken up, and reshipped to stores in that particular marketing area.

The opposite happens, too. A company may ship its products to a central warehouse where a make-bulk operation occurs. The larger, more economical shipment is then transported to its destination.

Location of Warehouses

Warehouses must be located with certain considerations in mind. Because of shipping costs, distances from the point of manufacture to major markets or points of distribution must be taken into consideration. This is the reason for the make-bulk warehouse and the break-bulk warehouse. In both cases, shipments can be rearranged so that their next shipment can be put in the most economical form.

Another important consideration in locating the warehouse is the cost of the warehouse itself and the materials-handling system it uses. New methods of materials handling are constantly being introduced, including automation. Your materials-handling system and your warehouse size must be matched for the most economical result.

Order Processing and Inventory

The order-processing and inventory-control functions are literally the heart of the distribution system. *Order processing* involves receiving orders from customers, recording and billing, and putting the order together for shipment. It is a job that must be done quickly and accurately. As stated before, distribution is a continuous process: goods flow out and orders flow in. The order-processing department exercises control over that flow.

Inventory control involves supply. It is useless to process orders if the goods aren't there. Inventory control is a feedback information system that keeps track of the supplies on hand and warns when the supply of an item falls below the shortage point. While stores may make an inventory count seasonally, a manufacturing concern with a free-flowing distribution pipeline must have continuous information that is regularly updated.

10

Have You Hugged
Your Wholesaler
Lately?

In the previous section we discussed how goods are moved in familiar ways such as trucks, railroads, planes, and ships and barges. Now we are going to examine another side of distribution: the role of the middleman.

Middlemen also help to move goods from the manufacturer's loading platform to the place where they are purchased. These people are known as middlemen because they act as intermediaries in helping the product on its journey.

You will see that there are a number of routes that can be chosen for this journey. Aptly enough, marketing people refer to these routes as channels of distribution because goods flow along a well-known channel.

Middlemen are businesspeople whose organizations perform various tasks and services for which they are paid. Thus, it is said that they add value to the product. This chapter covers some of these middlemen, the ways in which they operate, and how to identify them according to the ways they do business.

FIVE WAYS TO GET PRODUCTS
TO YOUR CUSTOMERS

The Traditional Marketing Channel

Usually we think of the distribution channel as proceeding from manufacturer to wholesaler to retailer and finally to consumer. The wholesaler middleman provides the essential means of redistributing the goods he has received from the manufacturer.

Can you imagine what would happen if Colgate Palmolive had to deal with each of the thousands of stores that carry their toothpaste? Or, if the druggist had to deal with an individual salesperson from every manufacturer of every item on his shelves? Fortunately for Colgate and the druggist, there are drug wholesalers who divide this task into a convenient, manageable size. Colgate finds it quite possible to handle the orders from its wholesaler-customers. And the wholesalers' sales representatives are well equipped to handle quickly and efficiently the orders from their retailer-customers.

If you look at the yellow pages of your telephone book under "Foods," "Drugs," or "Hardware," you will see the proportion of wholesalers (or brokers) to retailers of that particular field in your community. Without this dividing up of the distribution task, many manufacturers would face a very difficult problem.

The Manufacturer-to-Consumer Channel

There are some manufacturers that choose to skip the middleman entirely. Kirby Vacuum Cleaners, for example, is quite successful in selling direct to the consumer. Perhaps you've had the Avon Lady call on you, or you have attended a Tupperware party. In each case, you were dealing directly with the manufacturer's representative. This kind of distribution, however, represents a very small percentage of the total sales in the United States.

The Manufacturer-to-Agent-to-Consumer
Channel

There is another route which is particularly common in the industrial field. Manufacturers, particularly smaller ones, often have agents in the field who sell and take orders for them from industrial firms. These agents may or may not have stocks on hand.

In marketing, when we talk about *agents* and *merchant wholesalers*, we are talking about two different kinds of middlemen. They divide themselves into two broad categories: the agent wholesalers and merchant wholesalers. The difference is that agents don't usually own the products they handle, while merchant wholesalers do; the merchant wholesaler has "taken title to the goods."

Manufacturer-Retailer-Consumer Channel

Some manufacturers set up their own retail outlets and supply them directly. For example, Sherwin-Williams Paint Company owns its own stores and markets the Sherwin-Williams-labeled paint through them. But Sherwin-Williams also makes paint that it sells to wholesalers under a different label. Mary Carter Paints also has its own stores, but these are franchise operations, not wholly owned.

Manufacturer-Distributor-Wholesaler-Retailer Channel

Sometimes a product will move through three parties before reaching the customer. Particularly when distribution is widespread and there are many outlets, a few large distributors will service the wholesalers. The wine business provides interesting examples of both the traditional channel and the added distributor.

A wine wholesaler in your city probably purchased his stock of domestic wines, say Gallo, directly from the vineyard. But his imported wines, such as Barton & Gustier (B&G), have passed through a third party, a négociant. He has purchased the wine from the French vineyards, blended it, bottled it, and labeled it. He then shipped this product to the wholesaler.

Industrial Distribution

We have already mentioned the agent in an industrial channel. There is more than one kind of agent. Industrial products present a special case since so many go directly from producer to manufacturer.

MIDDLEMEN COME IN SIZES— HOW TO GET THE RIGHT FIT

The ways products can make their way from producer to consumer have just been described. You now know that different combinations of intermediaries may be encountered in the distribution channel— agents, brokers, wholesalers, retailers—before the consumer touches the product. You also learned that there are two broad categories of middlemen, agents and wholesalers, and how to distinguish between them on the basis of ownership of product.

Now you are going to learn about some of these agents and wholesalers and how to distinguish among them on the basis of the way they perform their tasks.

Full-Service Wholesalers

When we speak of wholesalers, this is the type that usually comes to mind. A company that carries a line of abrasives, belts, and pumps for industrial use is a typical wholesaler. Wholesalers are different from other middlemen because they purchase the merchandise they distribute. They are further distinguished by the fact that they perform several important services for both customers (retailers or consumers) and suppliers (manufacturers and producers).

Wholesaler Services.   The wholesaler makes a profit on the goods he handles. This profit is justified by the service he performs as an intermediary in the distribution channel. Let's examine some wholesaler services.

1. *Selling.* We have already noted how important this service is to the manufacturer. The wholesalers' salespeople reach all possible outlets to sell the producer's product.

2. *Purchasing.* While most large industrial firms employ purchasing specialists, many retail firms cannot. Even buyers for large department stores rely on the help and advice of resident buyers or buying offices. Wholesalers perform this purchasing function for hundreds of thousands of retailers. They not only know *what* to buy, but *when* to buy. They are the retailer's cushion against inventory shortages or overstock. They make it possible for the retailer to deal with one sales representative, rather than dozens.

3. *Transporting.* Wholesalers operate within limited, well-defined territories that they know as well as the back of their hand. They are dedicated to fast, efficient delivery, or fast, efficient servicing of their customer's transport. In an emergency, the retailer knows he can request and have delivery of needed merchandise, sometimes within minutes.

4. *Warehousing and handling.* Overly large, expensive inventories could clog both retailer's and producer's shelves if not for the wholesaler's warehousing facilities. Moreover, wholesalers have the equipment to break up bulk shipments from the producer to smaller sizes for shipment to retail customers.

5. *Credit and merchandise responsibility.* The wholesaler takes over a large billing and credit-extending responsibility. In addition to extending credit to customers, the wholesaler reduces delinquent accounts by knowing customers and their financial accountability. By taking title to the products, the wholesaler lifts worries about potential loss due to fire, theft, spoilage, or sudden shifts in demand from the shoulders of *both* producer and retailer.

THE RACK-JOBBER WHOLESALER.   There are special merchant wholesalers known as *rack-jobbers.* They fill a need created by the expanding merchandising of various products in the big chain food and drug stores. The rack-jobber sets up counters or racks (in effect a small department) and takes over the entire responsibility for operating it. The rack-jobber operation most familiar to you probably is the paperback book or the newspaper and magazine section in your local drugstore or supermarket.

Limited-Service Wholesalers

The traditional wholesaler performs a number of important services for producers and retailers. But there are several other wholesalers who do not provide all the services mentioned previously although they do take title to the goods.

CASH-AND-CARRY WHOLESALERS.   This wholesaler makes savings for customers possible by eliminating delivery and credit. Many lumber and building supply firms operate in this way. The builder sends his own truck around, picks up what he needs, pays for it with cash, and drives off. The warehouse employees who bring the merchandise out of stock will also aid the customer in loading.

TRUCK JOBBERS.   These wholesalers are sometimes known as wagon-jobbers from the old horse-and-wagon days. They service many retail stores and usually have a definite route. They make deliveries and take orders or sell merchandise direct. You've probably seen them parked in front of your neighborhood grocery or novelty store. They often carry lines such as candy, soft drinks, bakery goods, or dairy products. They render a special service to the small retailer dealing in perishables.

DESK JOBBERS.   Desk jobbers are also known as drop shippers because the transactions they arrange include a drop shipment—a shipment direct from producer to retailer. Though desk jobbers take title to their merchandise, they never actually handle it; thus, the warehousing function is eliminated. This is a particularly desirable feature when bulk or heavy products such as coal, lumber, and grain are involved.

Agent Wholesalers

Generally referred to as agents, these middlemen, as we have noted:

1. Do not take title (own) the goods they handle.
2. Perform fewer services and/or perform their services quite differently from the traditional limited-services or full-service wholesaler.

Let us review the major types and see how they function in the distribution-channel system.

BROKERS.   Brokers are typical go-betweens. They make the connection between someone who wants to sell and someone who wants to buy and help make the sale. They then take a commission from the seller for their services. Commissions are standard or accepted in many businesses such as food, real estate, or stocks and bonds. Usually these commissions are low, 2% to 3%. (But brokerage fees on Wall St. are negotiable.) However, if you open the door for an armaments manufacturer or a country-wide franchise, for example, your fee might be quite sizable.

SELLING AGENTS.   These agents often represent small manufacturers who have no marketing departments of their own. Many manufacturers producing special items used in industry—nuts and bolts, machine-tooled parts, industrial rubber goods—make use of a selling agent. Agents handle all the marketing problems for the firm they represent. They are regarded as a company employee and are compensated either by commission or salary.

MANUFACTURER'S AGENTS.   Unlike the selling agents, these are basically independent commission agents working within a restricted territory. A manufacturer may use one or more of them, and he may use them in conjunction with his own sales force. These agents handle a number of different noncompetitive lines, but they have little to say about marketing policy. Their most valuable service is reaching and aggressively selling markets the small manufacturer might not be able to reach and in opening up new markets for established products quickly and economically.

COMMISSION MERCHANTS.   We think of these middlemen in relation to products such as hogs, wheat, or cotton. They usually operate in a huge central market; the Chicago Board of Trade or Chicago Mercantile Exchange are notable ones. They take charge of the shipment, find a buyer, and complete the transaction at the most favorable price. They then deduct their commission on the basis of this price. Commission merchants are usually well-known and established firms in their particular field and are given considerable latitude by those they deal with.

FOOD BROKERS AND DISTRIBUTORS.   In the food field, it is necessary to distinguish between brokers and distributors. Generally speaking, food brokers act as manufacturers' representatives. They sell to retail food stores and take the place of a manufacturer's sales force. They do not take title to goods and usually drop ship. Food distributors, on the other hand, take possession, warehouse, and frequently deliver to stores and restaurants.

RESIDENT BUYERS.   These are independent agents who operate in a market such as furs or women's dresses. They charge a fee or commission on the sales they negotiate. Their knowledge is particularly helpful to buyers from out-of-town department stores. Do not confuse them with resident buying offices that are maintained in buying centers such as New York City's garment center by out-of-town department stores.

The Middleman Trade-Off

Many manufacturers treat their middlemen with the care and solicitude they would offer to a rich uncle since these people are the lifeline of the business. So, choose middlemen carefully, with attention to those that best fit your business.

Experiment. Don't get lost in a big, successful operation; a smaller (and hungrier) wholesaler may be the one for you. Get them to spell out exactly what services they can offer you. Maybe you don't need every single service. Since service is what you pay for, this is your chance to make a trade-off. In any case, remember these are people you will work with for years; make sure they are right for you.

CHOOSE A RETAILER AS YOU WOULD A SPOUSE

The last stop on the channel of intermediaries is the retailers who may have received their products from one or several of the wholesalers reviewed previously.

Let's review the types of retail outlets. They will be identified in terms of their services.

DEPARTMENT STORES.   These carry a variety of lines, often in the higher-priced categories. They offer expert sales help, charge accounts, delivery service, and promote their merchandise heavily, usually through newspapers.

CHAIN STORES.   These are prominent in the drug and food fields, feature a wide variety of items, and are often self-help stores. A&P is one of the largest. In the general merchandise field, Sears Roebuck and K-Mart are typical. These stores account for about one-third of all retail sales.

DISCOUNT STORES.   These are cash-and-carry operations originally featuring appliances and TVs but now in a variety of fields such as jewelry, food, clothes, and sporting goods.

FIGURE 7. Cash and carry wholesale operation.

SINGLE-LINE STORES AND BOUTIQUES.   Typical of every Main Street, these specialize in jewelry, books, hardware, or men's wear. *Boutiques* are special specialty stores carrying such items as jeans, costume jewelry, or shoes.

CONVENIENCE STORES.   These carry limited lines, often food and drug items. Self-service operations, they stay open late and are located closer to residential areas than main shopping centers are. 7-11 stores are typical of this type.

SHOPPING MALLS.   A grouping of a number of stores surrounded by a large parking area. Malls often merchandise themselves for the benefit of all their member stores. Usually a large department store serves as an anchor or focal point.

These are the major retail outlets that account for the bulk of retail sales. However, there are other interesting ways for the consumer to complete the last step in the distribution process.

11

Let's All Get Out
and Push!

HOW PRODUCTS ARE PROMOTED

Promotion is all around you. You can hardly escape it! Whether you are watching TV, driving to work, flipping through your favorite magazine, or just walking through a store, you are bound to encounter promotion for a product or a service.

First, let's define some terms that often cause confusion. Marketing people use the term *promotion* in several different ways.

Promotion is the overall term for all activities that contribute to the sales success of a product or service. For example, a marketing director might ask "What kind of promotional activity are you planning to put behind this product?" He wants to know what kind of advertising you are planning to run, what kinds of cartons you are going to use, or if you are going to include a dish towel in every box of detergent.

A *promotion* usually refers to a planned program of activities designed to increase the sales of a given product or service. A promotion can be when your nearby shopping plaza puts on a season-end special sale in which all the stores stay open until midnight and calls it a "Midnight Madness Special." Note that the promotion also includes advertising which may be on radio or TV, come in the mail, or appear in the local paper.

Promotional materials are anything of a physical nature involved in a promotion. Display pieces on counters, posters on windows, and cartons that can be made into displays are among all the possible promotion pieces. Companies that sell promotional material have catalogues. Look at your pen or pencil. Does it bear the name of a bank or insurance company? Who sent you the calendar on the wall?

Point of purchase, or P.O.P., is another name for the promotional material you find in stores. Other examples of this are cigarette or candy displays at checkout counters.

A *dealer promotion* is one in which the dealer or store puts on the promotional activity for the dealership or store. A *manufacturer's promotion* is one in which the maker of the product puts on a promotion for the benefit of his dealer. An example is when the detergent manufacturer puts a dish towel in every box and advertises the free offer on the outside of every box.

The Promotional Mix

As you see, different people may mean different things when they refer to promotion. Let's take the most general one, the promotion the marketing director was talking about when asking, "What kind of promotional activity are you planning?"

We can break this down into some well-recognized parts:

ADVERTISING.   Paid-for promotion which conveys a selling message by means of media—newspapers, TV, radio, magazines, and outdoor or poster advertising.

PUBLICITY.   Unpaid-for messages, usually in the form of news stories or articles reflecting favorably on the company, its products, or its services.

SALES PROMOTION.   These are activities other than publicity and advertising by which we seek to increase the sales of goods and services. Here you find the planned promotion as well as the promotional materials.

We are now going to examine each of these aspects of promotion more closely. Together, they form the *promotional mix*. Just as with the marketing mix, the marketing director must decide how he or she will employ each segment of the mix.

THE ADVERTISING PART OF PROMOTION

Most marketing people distinguish between advertising and promotion in their minds and budgets even though, as has been pointed out, promotion is the proper umbrella term for all promotion activities. Most big marketers have advertising budgets that include costs of media advertising—advertising that appears on TV and radio, in newspapers and magazines, or on billboards. Anything else—promotional materials and activities of all kinds—falls within the promotion budget. Marketers such as Pepsi Cola or General Mills are big advertisers; they seem to be everywhere. But most of us are not aware that their promotional budgets may be almost as great as their advertising budgets.

First, let's examine the advertising side of the overall promotional picture.

Four Kinds of Advertising Departments

It is possible for you to walk into four different buildings in your town and be directed to the Advertising Department. Each one of them would be different. Let's begin by defining them.

NEWSPAPER AND MAGAZINE ADVERTISING DEPARTMENTS. These are occupied by salespeople, the men and women who call on advertisers and solicit their advertising business for their publishers. They are selling space just as advertising representatives for radio and TV stations are selling time.

DEPARTMENT STORE ADVERTISING DEPARTMENTS.   These departments prepare advertising only for the store's products, and they do it fast. That's why department stores have ad departments—so they can get advertisements for their goods into the hometown newspapers as soon as possible.

CHAIN STORES.   These stores also have their own advertising departments. Here personnel put together the ads promoting dozens of items at your chain supermarket or weekend specials at Woolco's or Sears.

CORPORATE ADVERTISING DEPARTMENTS.   These departments have a supervisory and managerial function. Practically all marketing companies of any size have an advertising department with an advertising director who oversees the budget and the work done by the company's advertising agency. These advertising agencies are primarily responsible for deciding where their client's promotional advertising dollars should be spent and how the selling story should be presented to the public. It is an awesome and vital responsibility. The fate of the product may rest on the performance of the advertising agency. A weak advertising campaign can cause the product to fail.

Well, what *is* an advertising agency? What is it made up of and how does it work?

The Services in a Full-Service Advertising Agency

The full-service advertising agency consists of a group of many skilled specialists. Their specialized efforts are combined to produce successful advertising. While there are about 6,000 advertising agencies in the United States, only about 200 of them handle multimillion-dollar advertising budgets for national advertisers whose names are so familiar to you. Most of these agencies are located in New York City; this is why Madison Avenue has come to mean advertising.

But what about the other 5,800 agencies, several of which may be in your hometown? They handle the advertising and promotion for all the thousands and thousands of marketing enterprises that aren't among America's four or five leading brewers or bakers or cigarette makers. Nor are all of them full-service agencies. Some consist of three or four persons who may each perform several of the tasks performed by a single person or single department in the full-service agency. We can break down the agency's performance by functions.

ACCOUNT MANAGEMENT.   An agency regards each marketing company it serves as an account. Each account has one or more account managers or account executives. His or her job is to oversee the operation of the agency people on the account. He or she is the primary contact between agency and client. The corresponding person in the client's organization is the advertising manager or executive in charge of the corporate advertising department.

CREATION OF ADVERTISING.   Two separate departments in the agency are primarily responsible for making the ads, commercials, and posters you see promoting various products. They are the copy and the art departments.

Copywriters are more than people who simply write copy or think up slogans. It is the copywriter's responsibility, using all the information he or she can gather, to discover the most interesting and saleable features of the client's product and to present them in a hard-hitting and convincing selling story.

The art director works closely with the copywriter. It is his or her job, after the selling story has been written, to design and plan the appearance of the ad so that it will be attractive and eye-catching to consumers. Layouts are made in stages from roughs to finishes.

BUYING AND CHOOSING MEDIA.   The media department is responsible for choosing the media—newspaper, radio, TV, magazine, and outdoor—by which the client's advertising will reach the public. They are also responsible for contracting with the media for time and space and deciding how much of the client's budget will be charged to each one. Media selection is an important and difficult task. The media department must match the profile of the client's target markets with the profiles of the media's audience. Just as products have market segments with definite profiles, so every advertising medium appeals to a group of people with a unique profile.

PREPARING PLATES AND ENGRAVINGS.   The print production department of the agency is responsible for ordering the type and engravings which make up the final plate from which the advertisement is printed.

RADIO AND TV PRODUCTION.   Large agencies have a radio and TV director who supervises the production of commercials. Television commercials are seldom produced by the agencies themselves; usually they use outside sound and film production studios who have the costly equipment and the expert knowledge required to make commercials. If you are a small business with a limited advertising budget, note that radio and TV stations often can provide low-budget commercials for you, prepared in their own studios.

MARKETING AND ADVERTISING RESEARCH.   Full-service agencies have the people to supervise or carry out research assignments. This may be the kind of market research with which you are familiar, or it may be research into the effectiveness of media and advertising.

MARKETING SERVICES.   Most full-service agencies have people who are knowledgeable in marketing. They work directly with the client's marketing people.

OTHER SERVICES.   In addition to the usual departments necessary to operate any business such as accounting and personnel, large agencies have test kitchens, TV viewing studios and model stores and test publications for the benefit of their clients.

How Agencies Charge Their Clients

There are three usual methods used by agencies to charge their clients for their services.

THE 15% SYSTEM.   All recognized agencies are eligible to receive what amounts to a 15% commission on all advertising time and space purchased for client's accounts through the agency. The agency bills its clients for the stated cost of time and space and pays the media 85% of the total cost of time and space.

PRODUCTION CHARGES.   Agencies usually charge a 17½% commission when billing their clients for artwork, type, and engravings purchased by the agency in producing a print ad. This 17½% is often tacked on for any outside service purchased by the agency on behalf of its clients.

FEES.   A few of the large agencies will handle an account for an agreed upon fee. One reason for this is that the agency may be discouraged from placing all the client's advertising appropriation in commissionable media. Smaller agencies, whose clients may have need for nonmedia advertising, often use the fee system from necessity. Others work for a stated fee, charging the difference between that fee and the income from commission-paying media.

PEOPLE WHO CAN HELP YOU

In most cities in which marketing and promotional activities are carried out, there are a number of services that support the advertising agencies.

PRINTING.   Most cities have printing plants with services that range from small letterpress job printers to high-speed four-color press-

FIGURE 8. A 1250 offset duplicator press. This is the press used by almost all small job printers.

es. It is important for an agency to know which printer should be used for a particular job. A small job printer can do a perfectly satisfactory job on letterheads, announcements, and business cards. But for an elaborate four-color brochure or annual report, you would require a printer with four-color presses and skills in art, mixing of inks, and proofreading.

TV PRODUCTION STUDIOS. As mentioned earlier, TV commercials are generally produced by independent studios. These studios tend to be concentrated in New York and on the West Coast. Florida and Texas are popular with TV producers, too.

The production of a TV commercial can cost from a few hundred to thousands of dollars. The TV commercials for marketing nationally distributed packaged goods are produced by studios with all the equipment and expertise to make a full-length feature film. Your particular TV job may not be this demanding. A simple commercial for a local advertiser can be made by the staff of the local TV station, using their own cameras, director, and studio time.

RECORDING STUDIOS.   Many cities have recording studios such as you might associate with the making of a pop record. They often have 8-track stereo equipment and engineers to mix the sounds. They can record radio commercial tapes for you, as well as the sound tracks for audio-visual presentations.

ART STUDIOS.   Graphic art studios are important to both advertisers and their agencies. Smaller agencies often do not have their own art directors and have their layouts (advertising designs) done for them by an art studio (they bill their clients for the service). Art studios will also do any other kind of graphic work such as preparing sales presentations, designing trademarks, doing package design, or designing letterheads.

COMMERCIAL ARTISTS AND PHOTOGRAPHERS.   Commercial illustrators and photographers are also useful to advertising and marketing people. While painted and drawn illustrations are not as

FIGURE 9. Sound studio with 18-track console. Here the operator mixes the sounds. These sound studios are often used when making radio commercials with sound backgrounds.

FIGURE 10. Outdoor advertising art studio with sign being prepared for painting from a design supplied by the client. This is a "painted board," different from the more common "24-sheet poster" which is made from printed paper. Look closely at the bottom left and you can see the divisions between the panels. When the painting is finished, the panels will be disassembled, trucked to the site, and put back together.

popular as they once were, great improvements have taken place in cameras, film, and photography. A photographer from the local newspaper can often do a good job for you. Stock art (pictures of a wide variety of situations purchased from a catalogue) is also available at modest prices.

FREE-LANCE WRITERS. Many times an agency or company with a special assignment will call upon a free-lance writer to perform the job for them. An engineering firm, for example, may call in a writer to give editorial supervision for a written presentation. Free-lancers are sometimes used as speech writers or are called upon to prepare annual reports. Most art studios and printers know where to obtain free-lance writing.

110

WHAT IF J. WALTER THOMPSON WON'T TAKE YOU?

Remember, the preceding discussion was about the activities of a full service agency. What about the thousands of other agencies around the country (the ones you are most likely to deal with) who serve local and regional businesses?

The account executive may write copy after having done the necessary research with the aid of the receptionist. Many smaller agencies do not retain a full-time art director; instead, they farm out their artwork to an art service. Most cities of over 100,000 will have several good ones. The agency may also rely on local stations or sound studios to create commercials for it. It is also quite possible for it to retain outside specialists to make up media plans. Thus, the job gets done. However, if you are the client with a small business of your own, it also requires close supervision on your part.

Picking a Local Agency

The agency you are going to deal with will have a few people—maybe only two or three—who put on different hats at different times. Which agency can do the best job for you?

Of course, this depends a great deal on what your needs are. If your work is mainly promotions and display, you'll need a proven "idea person." If you want regular newspaper ads, you'll want to look for an agency with a clever writer.

You can start your search by talking to knowledgeable people around town: art services, media salespeople, businesspeople like yourself. Ask, "Who do you think would do the best job for me?"

Go to the agencies. Take a look at their offices. Do they look professional and well-established, no matter how small? Meet the people in the office and find out what they do. Ask for a list of their clients. Who do they work for and how long have they worked for them? Call up a couple of these clients and ask them how they get along with their agency. Do they have experience on accounts similar to yours? Who specifically would work on your account? What sort of fees do they charge?

Don't choose an agency because you know the owner. Don't choose an agency with accounts considerably larger than yours (your business won't receive the attention it deserves). Don't choose an agency because it is old and established (the young, ambitious one may be able to do a better job for you).

Do sit down with the agency people, explain your business and problems to them, and try to detect if they are truly interested and even excited about working with you.

Lastly, remember that you may not need an agency at all. It's quite possible you can get your promotional job done by using those services already discussed: printers, studio reps, sound studios, free-lance writers, and others.

THE PROMOTION PART OF PROMOTION

The promotion budget can be invested in a number of ways. Here are some of the major ones.

Displays

When you see merchandise displayed in a store or store windows, you are looking at what marketers call "display material." Most marketers supply their dealers with such display units. The best way to understand displays is to look around in your supermarket. You will find displays of every size, shape, and variety. The store manager may have

FIGURE 11. End of aisle display supplied by product manufacturer.

FIGURE 12. Store manager replenishes a wine unit display provided by the wholesaler. This display is at the end of the aisle in the most favored wine department position.

taken some bottles and cans and built them into a pyramid. That's a display. You will find odds and ends piled into a shopping cart or basket. That's a jumble display, intended to give the impression of a throw-away bargain. A shipping carton has been cut open and the top and sides folded back in an ingenious way to provide a display case for the contents. These are posters on the walls, display cases that revolve, mobiles that hang from the ceiling, and strips on the edges of the shelves. All of these are displays.

Dealer Promotions

Dealer promotions are events—often *sales* events—put on by an individual retail store. A promotional event has a theme and a reason behind it. Holidays such as Thanksgiving, Christmas, and Easter are events. So is back-to-school time. Retailers, as you have often seen, tie in with these events.

A promotion must be carefully scheduled and coordinated. Merchandise must be ordered, department decoration arranged for, window display space reserved, and advertising scheduled. Everything must be in place on the opening day of the promotion.

There are literally hundreds of ideas for promotions. New ones and variations of old ones keep popping up all the time.

Manufacturer Promotions

If you examine the cereal box on your kitchen shelf, you will discover that if you send in two boxtops and a couple of dollars, the company will send you a baseball autographed by all the members of your favorite big league team. This promotion helps the sales of cereal and thus aids the retailer. Customers are encouraged to "pull" the product off the shelves, while the manufacturer's salesperson is aided in "pushing" the product into the store. The number of these promotions scheduled by the manufacturer will often have considerable influence when the manufacturer's sales representatives call on the retail trade.

The use of a gift such as a baseball, towels, or glassware involves what is known as a premium. When the cost of the premium is covered by the money you send in with the boxtops, the premium is known as a self-liquidating premium. Coupons are a form of premium.

Sweepstakes, Contests, and Shows

Sweepstakes and contests are also put on by manufacturers to help increase the demand for their product. One of the advantages of the sweepstake or contest is that it keeps the entrant buying the product over a period of time as one of the requirements of eligibility. Fashion shows and demonstrations of various kinds may also be staged by the manufacturer to promote sales.

Personalities

A marketer or his agency will frequently retain a personality to represent his company. These spokesmen or spokeswomen may be well-known figures from the sports world or from the theater. You have seen O.J. Simpson rushing through the airport on behalf of Hertz Rent-a-Car, Bruce Jenner winning a gold medal at the Olympics because he trained on Wheaties, and Jane Russell demonstrating how a Playtex 18-Hour Bra helps to control a full figure.

Sometimes these people will make personal appearances at stores and lectures, give advice, or simply sign autographs. Anyone who is an expert or an authority, whether in cooking, skiing, or make-up, is sure to attract a crowd.

Co-op Advertising

As the name indicates, this is a joint venture. Usually the manufacturer supplies the ads or commercials. They are prepared by the sponsor's agency and are high quality. These are made available to retailers on a shared-cost basis. You've seen many of them. A TV commercial with retailers listed at the end in "Available at . . ." is co-op. A newspaper ad for a nationally distributed brand with dealers' names in the bottom inch is another form.

Nice Guy Advertising

Sometimes a company does not want to convey a selling message about the product. Rather, it wishes to get across an idea about something else. This goes by various names: corporate, institutional, or advocacy advertising.

Frequently corporate advertising is designed to make the public think well of the company. The company's good image, the regard with which it is held, is important to any business.

Public Service Advertising

Another form of advertising which seeks to gain goodwill for the company is advertising in the public interest. In this form, the company lends its support to a good, popular, or worthwhile cause. Frequently, support for the causes will be of direct or indirect benefit to the company.

The Federal Communications Commission requires that TV and radio stations devote a certain percentage of their time to "public service" commercials.

THE ADVERTISING COUNCIL.   The Council started during WW II as a means of directing advertising's skills in aiding the war effort. Today it contributes campaigns to a number of public service efforts. "Smokey the Bear" is one of its famous ideas.

SMALL BUSINESS INSTITUTIONAL ADVERTISING.   The big advertising budgets of the large corporations make it possible for them to put their ideas and causes before the public. Can local or regional businesses do the same thing? Sure they can! For example, when a new football coach was to be introduced at a local "Quarterback Club," a number of local businesses banded together and bought a full-page ad in the local newspaper encouraging people to attend the reception and demonstrate their support for the school and its new coach. Many of the school's alumni reside in the city, and the sponsor's names were prominently displayed in the ad. Or, look at the outfield fence where the Little League or American Legion teams meet. You'll see painted signs advertising a dozen or more local businesses. This is great public service advertising.

PUBLIC RELATIONS— GETTING A MILLION DOLLARS WORTH OF FREE PROMOTION

You have just seen how, using space or time purchased from the media, a company may project its point of view or gain favorable notice. Now we are going to examine another means to accomplish the same end. In this, the elements of newsworthiness or entertainment make it possible for us to gain publicity. Let's see how this works.

Publicity vs. Advertising

Advertising is a definite message in a definite amount of purchased time and space. Publicity, on the other hand, usually comes in the forms of a news story or an article of general interest.

The media usually accept paid-for advertising. But they exercise considerable latitude in selecting and publishing news and articles. The content of the story, the inherent news or interest, is important to the editor.

The Forms of Publicity

MAGAZINE ARTICLES.   Magazine articles, particularly in the trade press (magazines devoted to the interests of one trade group, such as steel) are widely used. In fact, a trade or professional magazine could hardly be published without stories about its members and, therefore, publicity.

A recent issue of *Progressive Grocer*, for example, carried two stories which must have made the subjects very happy. "A Rich Little Super Makes Every Inch Count" is about Black's Market in Contra Costa County near San Francisco. The other concerns Les Jablonski, a small chain operator from Oakville, Missouri. These stories illustrate that the small business can get its share of national publicity.

Some articles are inspired or originate in the company that will benefit by them. Some, such as the *Progressive Grocer* stories, are done by the publication's editors. Often a free-lance writer will see a story in a company's activity and get its help in putting it together.

NEWS RELEASES.   A news release is a story which is released or sent out from the P.R. (Public Relations) department of an organization. It conforms to the same rules as any other news in the publication. It should have a news angle, and it should take the traditional reporter's Who, What, When, Where, How, and Why form. Often it is on a special release form used by the company and gives a desired release date and states who may be contacted for further information. The subject matter of a news release can be almost anything concerning your company as long as it is of news interest to the paper's readership.

When Volkswagen decided to build a new plant to assemble cars in Westmoreland County, Pennsylvania, it was a story of nationwide interest. It was front-page news in the Philadelphia and Pittsburgh press, to say nothing of the Westmoreland press.

INTERVIEWS AND NEWS CONFERENCES.   Stories favorable to the company are often gained through interviews and news conferences. When a professional football team selects a new coach, it often calls a news conference to "introduce" him. Sportswriters and announcers for the leading newspapers, stations, and news services will often be invited to lunch at a popular restaurant. The club's P.R. people will distribute a release containing much useful information.

PHOTOGRAPHS.   This is an often-neglected side of publicity. But it is a device many companies, particularly smaller ones, could well exploit. There are many low-budget, publicity-hungry city zoos around the country. Wait until spring comes and the baby chimps, hippos, and zebras are born. Editors fight for photographs!

SPONSORSHIPS.   The sponsoring of contests and events has become increasingly popular. Companies lend their names and financial backing to golf and tennis tournaments and auto and horse races. Local and regional businesses find sponsoring bowling, softball, and baseball teams is a good way to build a fine community image as well as attain publicity.

COMPANY PUBLICITY AND PRODUCT PUBLICITY.   You want to be sure to distinguish between company public relations and product public relations.

Company public relations came first. When muckrakers were revealing sins of the great corporations, big business began making an effort to improve its image in the public eye. Thus were born the first public relations counselors—men like Bernays and Ivy who advised corporations and their offices on their relations with the public.

Product publicity came along later. This is the free space or time obtained in the media by commercial products. For example, the food page in your paper may carry a story on baking and include a mention of a specific cake mix—that's product publicity. Food editors are bombarded daily with press releases from food growers and packagers.

An interesting aspect of product publicity is the effort made to get sight publicity for products in motion pictures and television shows. When the hero reaches into the refrigerator for a cold can of beer, it has to be somebody's brand. It might as well be yours.

How To Get Your Product Publicized

Let's say you are a small, new company and don't have a high-powered agency or public relations director working for you. How do you get a free ride for your company and your product?

First, become known by the writers for the business section of your paper. Send them a note telling them who you are and what you are doing. Write a letter of appreciation for a story they have done. Volunteer some information or a lead that might be helpful.

Have a press release form made up. If you want to know what they look like, your business writer will oblige you with an armload. Get a local art studio or printer to design one for you.

WRITING THE RELEASE.   Remember a release is a news story, not a boast. Your story should have an interesting angle to it, the type of thing the paper's readers will go for.

Sometimes it's best to call the newsroom first. Say, "Here's something that has just turned up here in our laboratory, and I thought it might interest you. If you think there is a story, I'll get the facts together and send them over to you."

Remember, too, that good works make good news. Most businesspeople have a well-developed sense of community responsibility. They serve on committees, take part in charitable drives, and devote time to worthy causes. All this is not without its rewards. When stories about drives and causes appear, the participants' names are often mentioned—together with their business connections.

Another point to keep in mind is that although hundreds of companies are competing for that free space, you are the local one, and editors are always looking for a local angle.

THE TRADE PRESS.   No matter what kind of business you are in, there is a trade publication devoted to the interests of your particular activity. Subscribe to it, make contact with its publishers, and note the kind of articles it publishes. These are pure publicity in most cases since they concern activities in your trade or profession. Can you come up with a story that might interest them?

12

Who's Minding
the Store?

You have seen that goods and services travel a diverse and sometimes long route. Ultimately most end up in a store.

This retail outlet, where we buy the necessities of daily living, is a mini-marketing world all of its own. As such, it deserves our close attention for retailing, the business of satisfying the needs of consumers, has a whole set of problems that are particularly its own. There are retailing decisions that have to be made regarding product, packaging, pricing, promotion, and, of course, distribution.

To help you understand how these retailing marketing mix problems are met and solved, we are going to take several steps. First, we are going to look at the background development of retailing.

Then we will examine retailing as it is today and might be in the future. Next we will see how retailing operates internally, how retailers organize themselves to meet retailing marketing problems of product, price, promotion, packaging, and distribution. Finally, we will examine the bottom line—how the retail store makes a profit.

THE MORE RETAILING CHANGES ...
PLUS C'EST LA MEME CHOSE

The retail store where the consumer buys the product, the end of the distribution line, has existed for a long time. Here, in America, one of the earliest retailers was the pack peddler. Riding in his wagon or plodding beside his heavily-laden donkey, he called on isolated frontier homes with goods the homemaker prized such as needles, yarns, buttons, and notions.

Another form was the trading post where bearded miners swapped gold dust for bacon and beans. Probably the most romantic retailing form of all was the yearly fairs where the mountain men sold furs for ammunition, food, and trade goods.

Whenever a new town sprang up in America, a general store was sure to appear, probably the only one in town. It carried everything from bolts of cloth to musical instruments to harnesses and tools. As populations grew, county seats grew and became shopping centers. Stores began to specialize; drugstores, meat and grocery markets, and hardware stores appeared. On Saturdays, the sidewalks would be crowded, and the hitching posts would all be taken by farm wagons and buggies whose owners may have come as far as 20 or 30 miles to do the family shopping.

The advent of rural free delivery and parcel post in the early 1900's made it possible for isolated farm families to sit around the kitchen table and select mail-order merchandise from catalogues published by Sears Roebuck and Montgomery Ward.

Meanwhile, in Philadelphia, an imaginative retailer named John Wanamaker came up with another idea: a department store that sold many different kinds of items under one roof.

As America grew and changed, retail outlets grew and changed, too. Innovative businesspeople found new and profitable ways to serve the buying public. The catalogue mail-order house in Chicago, Sears Roebuck, grew and grew until today it has sales over $13 billion dollars a year. All told, there are probably about two million retail outlets in the United States, doing well over $500 billion in sales.

CHAIN STORES.   It may seem hard to believe, but the chain store is a relatively recent invention. Not until the 1930's did the idea of food chain stores begin to take hold. Sears established its first successful mail-order operation in 1891. Today, most communities have a J.C. Penney, F.W. Woolworth, or regional drug or food chain store.

DISCOUNT STORES.   The savings involved in reduced overhead through inexpensive location, self-service, and no store frills enabled some stores to offer merchandise at discount prices. These were often chains of limited-line merchandisers: jewelry, refrigerators, and TVs. One of the more interesting developments is discount food stores selling non-branded products (a can of soup is simply marked "Vegetable Soup"). Woolco and K-Mart are popular discount chains, offshoots of Woolworth's and Kresge's.

CONVENIENCE STORES.　Again, someone saw a need and filled it. The convenience store is a store where you can go to pick up needed food and drug items in a hurry. They try to place themselves nearer to residential neighborhoods than the supermarkets do. They stay open longer. They are relatively small and carry restricted lines of merchandise—only the most popular soap, bread, or toothpaste. They often have only one clerk and are self-help. They tend to charge higher prices, probably on the theory that people are glad to pay a little extra for faster check-out and for not having to go all the way to town.

FRANCHISE STORES.　You are very familiar with these, particularly in the food field: Kentucky Fried Chicken, McDonald's, Pizza Hut, Hana Ichiban. The franchiser rigidly controls every phase of the operation, often down to the minutest detail. The person operating the franchise outlet makes an initial investment, manages, and shares the profits according to an agreed-upon formula. Franchising has proved extremely attractive because it combines having your own business with low-cost supply, expert site selection, and the managerial know-how of the parent company acquired in establishing and supervising hundreds of stores.

LIMITED-LINE SPECIALTY STORES.　These are stores that specialize in one kind of product such as shoes or fishing tackle. Boutiques (French for shop or booth) are small specialty shops featuring jewelry or a special kind of men's or women's wear. The success of the specialty store often depends on the kind of merchandise featured, the personality and expertise of the owner or manager, and the interior decoration of the store. Stores sometimes score a success on this last feature alone. In Paris, for example, the design of boutiques has become an important architectural specialty.

LEASED DEPARTMENTS.　Discount and department stores will often lease space to operators who may have knowledge or ability not possessed by the store itself. Cosmetics, watch repair, photography, and insurance often fall in this category.

LEASED DEALERSHIPS.   These are much like franchises in that the company owns the property and receives a percentage of sales as rent. Oil company-owned service stations are typical of leased dealerships.

COMPANY-OWNED STORES.   Large companies such as Firestone Tire or Florsheim Shoes sell products of their own manufacture through their own stores.

SHOPPING CENTERS AND FRAGMENTED DEPARTMENT STORES. The shopping center with stores surrounded by a large parking area is a phenomenon of modern, mobile America. Automobile ownership, high-speed highways, and the suburban explosion gave birth to the shopping center. Relatively inexpensive land made it possible to recreate a downtown shopping area in what was once a cow pasture. Inner-city deterioration, city parking and transportation problems, and the flight to suburbia demanded this new retailing form. The modern shopping mall is not just a collection of stores, but is a carefully designed and operated entity under a single management.

The creation of the clustered shopping center has also resulted in the fragmentation of the traditional downtown department stores. Somewhat smaller versions, or fragments, of Macy's, Belknap's, or Marshall Field are represented in the suburban shopping center.

NON-STORE RETAILING.   Retail sales also may be made without the use of a store. Sales are often made via the telephone, particularly to customers with credit cards. Door-to-door sales, made famous by the Fuller Brush man and used by manufacturers of vacuum cleaners and books, can be a very profitable form of retailing. The in-home sale, typical of Avon and Tupperware, is a variation on door-to-door.

VENDING MACHINES.   Widely used in factories and schools, these machines are capable of handling a wide variety of merchandise automatically.

MAIL ORDER AND DIRECT MAIL SALES.   The wide use of credit cards and the lists of credit card owners have resulted in an increase in the dollar-volume of merchandise sold in this manner. Prices charged for direct mail items have increased dramatically. It was thought for many years that $10.00 was the limit for a direct mail piece of merchandise. Today, direct mail offers frequently are in the hundreds of dollars.

FIGURE 13. Here is a form of retailing seldom seen in this country, but very popular in Europe. The owner rents space for the trailer in a parking lot and sets out his display of merchandise. Note how the side of the trailer makes an excellent billboard. When business slows, he'll pack up and move to another town. The trailer has sleeping quarters as well as storage space for the merchandise.

WHAT IT TAKES TO MAKE A STORE

If you talk with the manager of your supermarket or the owner of a nearby clothing store, he or she will tell you that there is a great deal more to running a retail store than meets the eye; it isn't just a matter of stocking the merchandise and selling it. Thousands of retail establishments fold each year because their proprietors didn't do things right. Let's see what it takes to succeed.

HOW TO CHOOSE YOUR SPOT.   Before establishing a store in a certain location, the retailer has to make an estimate of volume of business. Big chains often have outside marketing consultants to do this job for them. Many factors are taken into consideration: for instance, traffic counts, number of salespeople in neighboring stores, and estimates of neighborhood family income. Salespeople, suppliers, and chambers of commerce can often supply useful information. Big chains, with past experience and sophisticated methods, usually do well in choosing sites. Burger King and Kentucky Fried Chicken seem to know what they are doing every time. The retailer who relies on guesswork usually gets into trouble.

To a great extent, what you sell will strongly influence your location. A farm equipment store can be on a highway far out in the country if farmers travel that route to market. A department store is usually located near other department stores. Food stores seek locations near residential neighborhoods.

THE TRAFFIC COUNT.   As mentioned this is a count of the number of people and the kinds of people who pass a given location at given times. High-traffic locations are not important to every store. Your store may depend on quality, not quantity. Fast food take-out stores look for areas of heavy home-going, after-work traffic, especially that of working women.

THE COMPETITION'S LOCATION.   This must be taken into consideration. Some stores cling together—seafood sellers on the waterfront, automobile dealers on a well-traveled highway, service stations

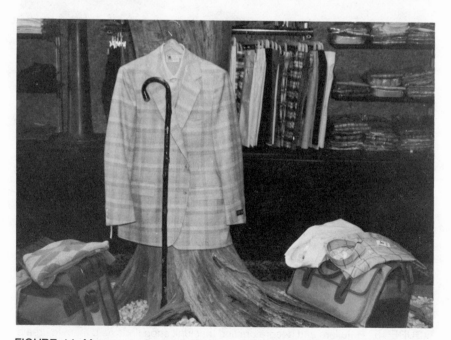

FIGURE 14. Menswear display built around the trunk of a dead tree. Retailers often give their stores character with imaginative interior decoration such as this.

at a popular intersection. Boutiques and specialty shops are often better off when they have an area to themselves.

TRAFFIC AND PARKING.   These are very important to most retailers. Unless the store is a special case, it must be easy and convenient to get to. Shopping centers have hurt stores in downtown locations on this point.

THE BUILDING AND ITS EQUIPMENT.   The front of the store, the entrance and windows, are important. Access should be easy and protect those inside against the weather. The windows are permanent ads and should be large and well-positioned. Seeing into the store is also important. When a see-through wall is used, the effect is that of a tremendously big and interesting window.

WHAT DOES YOUR STORE LOOK LIKE?   Store fixtures and equipment are all those items with which the retailer furnishes the inside of the store. They include shelves, counters, racks, display

FIGURE 15. Retailers and decorators find that junk shop finds help them to create good displays. This ancient meat scale is used here to show a selection of suspenders.

equipment, elevators and escalators, cash registers, and so on. Look at a women's clothing boutique and see how imaginative interior decoration and arrangement can be even in a small space. Illumination of stores ranges from bright, diffuse light in supermarkets to subtle indirect lighting in others. Today, few stores in any part of the country can afford to be without air conditioning. Interior layout is almost an art; trade publications, in the food field particularly, have devoted many pages to the subject.

Who's Going to Be Behind the Counter?

A retail store is a business organization and is subject to the same rules of organizing and staffing as any other business. A large department store may have a very complex organizational chart, whereas a small store will have fewer people carrying out such essential roles as Manager, Controller, Merchandise Manager, Credit Manager, Buyer, Advertising Manager, and Personnel Director.

PERSONNEL SELECTION.   Personnel selection is especially important to the retail store, particularly its sales personnel. After all, the salespeople are the first contact with the customer, often the *only* contact with the customer.

Department stores look for people who seem to have a merchandising instinct. Retailing is a queer and demanding business. It isn't for everyone. Look for the young man or woman who is going to love every minute of it—even if they have to work late on Christmas Eve and the merchandise manager is about to collapse from nervous exhaustion.

Ease and grace with people is essential. Sullen, impolite help have hurt more stores than they have realized. Personal honesty is vital, although it's hard to detect and much harder to come by. Remember, light-fingered personnel send hundreds of stores into the red each year.

BUYING MERCHANDISE.   For even the small specialty shops, buying merchandise for resale is a difficult and delicate task. The buyer must not only know the store's customers and their changing tastes and preferences, but also his or her sources of supply. A smart resident buyer (an independent professional buyer) can often help avoid costly mistakes.

Chains and supermarkets have a far more complicated problem. There may be as many as 6,000 different items on sale; some big chain drugstores have as many as 12,000! Purchasing on this scale requires the services of a number of buyers, each an expert in a special field. A grocery chain, for example, will have buyers of produce, meats, staples, and bakery goods. Chains often set up their own suppliers; a food chain may set up and buy the entire output of a grower of broilers. In addition, it may deal with a number of middlemen—wholesalers, brokers, and jobbers—mentioned in the chapter on distribution.

HANDLING MERCHANDISE.   Merchandise that has been purchased arrives at the retail store and is delivered to the receiving department. All incoming merchandise must be unpacked, checked against purchase orders, and recorded for inventory. Ticketing or price-marking is an important step. In a large food market, this may simply involve stamping the price on the package in indelible ink. In other stores, such as clothing outlets, the ticket must carry other information in addition to the price: size, color, fabric, and style number.

SALESMANSHIP.   The retail salesperson bears a big responsibility. Retail stores impress upon the salespeople that customers pay their salaries and should be treated accordingly. While some retailers, such as self-service supermarkets, discount houses, and vending machine operators, may regard personal retail salesmanship as unimportant, the salesperson is still very important to department stores and a host of smaller independent stores. He or she must be neat, clean, courteous, well-informed about the merchandise and the store's rules and policies, and schooled in the basic principles of closing the sale.

ADVERTISING.   Few major newspapers or independent radio stations could exist without the income derived from local retail advertising. Local chain and department stores are particularly heavy advertisers. Most have their own advertising departments within the store where their ads are written and designed. In the department store, speed is essential because merchandise managers wish to promote items as soon as possible. New items must be brought to the consumer's attention on an almost daily basis.

Chain food, drug, and general merchandise stores must prepare their own ads featuring dozens of items, including prices which are subject to change right up to the very last moment.

13

Have You Heard the One About the Problem-Solver and the Farmer's Daughter?

Now the captains and the kings have departed. The geniuses in the marketing department have done everything they could. Production has polished it until it shines. The advertising agency has knocked itself out producing sensational ads and commercials. The distribution pipelines are filled and the point of purchase material is in place. The fate of our product now rests with the sales force! It's a thought that makes many a marketing manager wake up in a cold sweat. Red Motley, a sales and marketing executive, put it quite neatly: "Nothing happens until somebody sells something."

So now we are going to look at those "somebodies" who have the ultimate responsibility of making it all pay off, of making the sale. We are going to look at their personalities and see if we can identify what makes them successful. We are going to identify the various kinds of salespeople and see how they operate in relating to their customers. Finally, we will examine how a salesperson goes about performing his or her job and how it all ties into the marketing process.

SALESPEOPLE ARE BORN *AND* MADE

If it were possible to identify the successful salesperson according to personal qualities, marketing managers would be very happy. Unfortunately we can't. All we know is that there are certain personal qualities the good salesperson must have. Without them, chances of success are much smaller. Let's look at some of these desired personal qualities.

Integrity. "To thine own self be true" is still good advice. The successful salesperson needs a strong sense of honesty and propriety toward his or her company, customer, and self.

Enthusiasm. You must believe in what you are doing. You must acquire the state of mind that looks forward to each day as a new challenge, a new opportunity to win.

Self-Confidence. Good salespeople do not believe only in what they are selling—they believe in themselves and their ability to perform. They expect to make the sale.

Imagination. Selling is a creative task. The salesperson's ability to think boldly and creatively is an important asset.

Poise. The good salesperson keeps control of the situation. Under stress, he or she must remain unflappable. Salespeople often run into upsetting situations, some deliberately created by others.

The Nature of the Job

A remarkable number of businesspeople begin their careers in sales. Today, especially, it is the royal road to the marketing department's executive suite. What are the good and bad points about a selling career?

Good: Selling allows you to be your own boss more than most jobs do. You can take yourself just as far and as fast as you are willing to extend your energies.

Bad: Many sales jobs keep people on the road for long periods of time. This is tough when you are young and raising a family. You get very tired of hotel food.

Good: The income from selling is almost unlimited, depending on what you sell and how well you sell it. Some people do quite well selling encyclopedias and cosmetics. Others do well selling diamonds or fighter planes. Others sell services.

Bad: Salespeople are sometimes victims of events beyond their control. Sources of income can dry up quickly when the economy goes into a slump.

Good: In selling, it's the bottom line that counts. For the persons who get results, few will question the color of their skin, where they went to school, or their sex. Many young women are selling successfully in businesses that might have been closed to them in past years.

The Kinds of Sales Jobs

In addition to retail salespeople, there are a great many other salespeople. It took only one person to sell you your motorcycle or car, but think of all the people it took to sell all the things that went into making your machine.

DIRECT SELLING.   There is a relatively small, but important, group of salespeople who sell the manufacturer's product directly to the consumer. They take on all the functions of the middleman themselves. Generally they work on a commission plus bonus basis. Sometimes they are awarded franchises or territories. Avon, Amway, and Tupperware are typical of this kind of operation.

Often these salespeople must deal with groups; this calls for the skills of a high-level professional in organizing the presentation. Their knowledge of the product line must be deep and complete. They must often be dexterous and clever demonstrators. Direct salespeople, who are given the opportunity to form and manage their own sales groups, frequently command remarkably high incomes.

WHOLESALERS REPRESENTATIVES.   The wholesaler's salespeople really represent two concerns. They work for their own employer, the wholesale house, and they also represent the manufacturers whose lines the wholesale house carries.

Wholesaler salespeople have a most important job in getting products into the number and kind of retail outlets that will best serve their clients (the manufacturers). A marketer of a line of medium-priced California wines would probably like to get into as many food and liquor stores as possible. But the manufacturer of a high-priced line of jogger's equipment would be quite particular about where his line was retailed.

Wholesaler salespeople often have a very intimate relationship with their customers. They check the store's inventory, rearrange displays, set up promotions, and fill orders. One of their most important jobs is to show retailers the manufacturer's promotion plan; this indicates the manufacturer's commitment to the retailer. They render real services to their customers and consequently have their trust and respect. Yet this close relationship with the customers does not mean that the salesperson does not function at the highest level of professional salesmanship.

MISSIONARY SALESPEOPLE.   As the name implies, these salespeople have a mission: to help stimulate sales for the benefit of both wholesaler and manufacturer. They are not so much interested in writing orders as they are in teaching techniques and installing devices that will make sales flow faster. They are often a combination of sales and promotion manager, adept at showing the retailer tested methods and procedures that will work for his particular product.

When a new line or product is introduced by a chain, they work to ensure its success by instructing and inspiring salespeople and store executives. Nor does the missionary salesperson's job stop there. For many weeks, he or she will call on the retail outlets, boosting morale, checking results, building new displays, and putting in new advertising campaigns and promotions. This type of salesperson is particularly active in the food and drug fields.

INDUSTRIAL SALESPEOPLE.   It probably took hundreds of salespeople to sell General Motors all the parts that go into one of its cars. Salespeople who represent companies that manufacture products used by other manufacturers are seldom seen or noticed. Yet, they are absolutely essential to the marketing process.

The big difference lies in the relationship between buyer and seller. It certainly is not one of gaining admission to an executive's office and inducing him or her to buy another insurance policy or to participate in a stock-purchase plan. Neither the industrial buyer nor seller wants it that way; rather, the ideal is a relationship of trust and confidence based on dependability and performance.

The purchasing agent and the industrial vendor need one another. The person responsible for purchases needs dependable suppliers of known, reputable products at competitive prices. The manufacturer's representative seeks to build a relationship that makes him almost a part of his client's operation. His or her goal is to be a problem solver whose products and expertise can help customers to overcome difficulties and operate more profitably.

Large manufacturing enterprises treat their suppliers with kid gloves from supplying them with phones for outside calls in well-appointed reception rooms to providing them with juice or coffee. Each sales representative is given a firm appointment, and the purchasing agent sets aside a reasonable amount of time for the interview. It's a long way from door-to-door personal selling!

RETAIL SALESPEOPLE.   You've probably had contact with a great many of these salespeople. Although they all work in a retail situation, there is a wide variety in their performance. Some, indeed, are clerks—order takers whose efforts don't extend further than asking "May I help you?" But, in most department stores and established,

successful retail stores, the salespeople are well-trained and knowledgeable.

Retail salespeople are close observers of human nature. Few
salespeople have a better opportunity to observe customers and their
human peculiarities since they meet dozens of people each day in
transactions that may take five or ten minutes to an hour or more.

Retail salespeople are trained in selling up (sometimes known
as related selling). If I buy a couple of shirts, the alert salesperson will
call my attention to the nearby tie rack and show me several ties that go
particularly well with my purchase. This ability to trade up a customer
is particularly important in the retail field because it can change a
store's whole profit picture. That related sale of tie-and-shirt was very
important; the profit margin on a $15.00 necktie is very wide!

Opportunities for progress and achievement in the retail field
are tremendous—particularly in department stores and in the chains
—via the sales route.

A LOT OF KNOWLEDGE GOES
A LONG WAY

Making a successful sale is not a case of playing it by ear or hitting a
lucky streak. A successful salesperson prepares for many long and careful hours just as a winning athlete does. The winners and successful
closers are those who have paid their dues.

Every moment of the salesperson's time is precious. It is up to
the salesperson and the sales manager to make sure that sales time is
utilized effectively through painstaking preparation and attention to
detail.

Product Knowledge

Knowing the product is an obvious requirement for a salesperson. He or
she must know about the product's design and materials, the results of
any tests on the product, and product performance capabilities under
various circumstances. These are all features, and they are very important.

There is, however, another kind of product knowledge that may
be much more important than product features or service. This is the
benefits your product can bring to your customer. It is worth your while
to make sure you understand the difference between the two kinds of
product knowledge. This differentiation lies at the heart of all selling.

Product Features Knowledge

A woman who sold in the better dresses section of a large department store once told me, "I always look carefully at the dresses displayed in the windows when I come to work in the morning. I know that those are the ones that are going to be inquired about most closely."

Your customers should have some questions about your product—it indicates that they are interested. You should be prepared to say, "I'm glad you asked me that." And you really should be glad, for this gives you the chance to expound on a desirable or interesting feature. Remember that enthusiasm is one of the outstanding characteristics of the successful salesperson. Enthusiasm comes from intimate knowledge of everything that is good, unique, or special about your product.

Product Benefit Knowledge

Features are those things manufacturers have done for themselves; these are the *reasons* the product performs as well as it does. *Benefits* are what the product does for the customer. Remember that we are most interested in ourselves and in what people are going to do for us.

Elmer Wheeler said, "Don't sell the steak, sell the sizzle"—one of the great slogans of marketing. It contains a great deal of truth. Mouth-watering anticipation sells steak. Will your product make me happier, or prettier, or richer, or more popular? As a salesperson, you better know just *how* it will perform this feat, because *that* is what I am going to buy—the *benefit!*

Customer Knowledge

The smart salesperson cases the prospect before ever meeting him or her. This is *personal* customer knowledge. What kind of a person is the prospect? What are his or her enthusiasms, hobbies, likes, dislikes, and background? All these facts come in handy as a salesperson develops a relationship with a new customer. When the customer is a company, the salesperson must have a good grasp of the company's operation, competitors, and industry.

BIRD-DOGGING
(SNIFFING OUT PROSPECTS)

There is a "80-20 rule" that all salespersons are familiar with. It says, in effect, that 80% of all sales come from 20% of all customers. Therefore, a salesperson is looking for those who fall in the 20% category.

How do you prospect or bird-dog? There are literally hundreds of ways, some of them peculiar to one particular kind of business. Here are several.

1. *Hidden Offers and Coupons.* Often a company will offer you a free booklet if you send in a coupon. You identify yourself as a prospect when, for example, you send for the brochure on "Ten Ways to Catch Giant Bass."

2. *Referrals.* This method is often used in personal selling. A satisfied customer recommends you to a new prospect, and the process begins. Sometimes it is known as the endless chain method.

3. *News Stories and Business Announcements.* Any change in business status may signal a selling opportunity. New offices or manufacturing plants offer leads. Wedding, engagement, and birth announcements are watched carefully by many salespeople.

4. *Government and Industrial Publications.* There are a number of published sources of lists of companies with their addresses, names of officers, type of business, and volume of purchases.

5. *Bird-Dogging.* When you buy a motorcycle, and the salesperson says, "Bring in a pal to buy one of these, and I'll rebate you $25.00 on your cost," that's bird-dogging.

PUTTING ON THE SHOW

A presentation is a somewhat more formal presenting of the sales story. Although it can be one-on-one, generally it involves one or more people from the vendor's company appearing before several people representing the prospect. In advertising, the new business pitch is a common form of sales presentation.

A presentation is basically a piece of show business. And, as in any performance, it demands meticulous timing and careful rehearsal. When several people are involved in making the presentation, lines must be rehearsed and parts understood. Lighting and props must be taken care of, too. Sound equipment that refuses to work or slide projectors that show pictures upside-down and backwards can destroy any presentation. Here are some of the physical selling tools that are used in presentations.

1. *Flip Charts.* These may be book-size, A-frames with flip-over pages or larger easel-type pages for larger audiences. They are primarily used to reinforce the speaker's reference to selling arguments and figures, as well as product illustrations.

2. *Audiovisuals.* These range from something as simple as a sound-and-slide film machine to closed-circuit television. In some cases, the entire presentation may be committed to film.

3. *Laboratory Results.* Results of independent tests are often used. These can be particularly impressive when an independent expert presents the findings.

4. *Models and Demonstrators.* If your product is a convenient size, it should be brought to the presentations. Cut-away models showing working parts are attention-getters. If clients can work the models, they can be particularly effective devices.

5. *Literature.* This includes brochures, booklets, and all printed material that can be left with the customer. Certainly this includes examples of advertising and promotion material, together with schedules and planned expenditures when available.

SORRY—WE JUST RAN OUT OF MIRACLES

Just as knights adventured after the Holy Grail and Spanish explorers sought a city where streets were paved with gold, so men and women have sought for a magic formula in selling. In an industrial society in which *system* is a watchword, why can't there be a foolproof system for successful selling?

Don't think that certain promotors haven't claimed to have found it. They've packaged it and sold it at a profit. You can buy magical waters from the Fountain of Youth, too!

No, there is no magic formula, no system that assures sales success. But there are basic selling principles that have emerged from millions of manhours of selling effort. These principles don't guarantee success. But their use does offer the salesperson some protection against failure. As such, they are well worth studying.

AIDCA

Remember that the formulas we are going to discuss are not the result of someone's stroke of genius. A salesperson did not wake up in the middle of the night and cry out, "I've got it! AIDCA—Attention, Interest, Desire, Conviction, Action!"

Rather, what occurred was a distillation of sales experiences, experiences that have led salespeople to see that yes, there *is* a pattern that runs through successful selling. It may not be magical, but it is certainly helpful. Sometimes it goes by the name of AIDCA. Sometimes it is called the Five Great Rules of Selling; sometimes we refer to it as the Idea Sequence Formula. Whatever we call it, it is the same, a distillation of what generally happens, in the course of a successful sale.

Why You Can Believe in the Route

Advertising and selling developed on parallel tracks. There was a time, however, when these tracks were very far apart. Before the modern marketing concept, great emphasis was put on selling. The salesperson was King or Queen. Advertising, on the other hand, was in a sad state. There was no science to it and no control over it. Much of it was wild, unsupported claims.

But a new breed of ad people entered the game and began to experiment. They put coupons in their ads and counted the results. When the coupon count went up, they continued what they did. As a result, their advertising worked better and better. One day a great light dawned on them: "Advertising is simply selling in print." They saw that mass selling and personal selling follow the same route time after time: gain attention, create interest, stimulate desire, impart conviction, and ask for the order. The salespeople smiled. They *always* knew that.

GETTING ATTENTION.   Getting attention may mean greetings from a receptionist or a nice response from a secretary. It also can mean attention so rapt that your prospect closes the door and asks his secretary to intercept all phone calls. People who have something important to say or something valuable to deliver get attention.

The other type of attention is intent listening. You literally have to make your customer prick up his ears. The good salesperson does it with words: "Mr. Jones, our study indicates that you may be overspending on paper clips by $5,000 a year." Or he or she may do it with gesture: "Just see how this inexpensive little gadget can peel, core, slice, dice, shoestring, or quarter a vegetable in 2 seconds flat!"

CREATING INTEREST.   Here's where we return to product benefits. Remember, nothing interests people as much as themselves. Your loose dentures don't interest me; *my* loose dentures do—very much. Therefore, the interest-seeking salesperson bores right into your self-interest—the particular need, want, or desire that concerns you most. For example, "You know, a pretty woman like you—it's a shame to have all those facial blemishes. Wouldn't you just love to have a clear, smooth complexion?"

STIMULATING DESIRE.   The psychology involved here is that if I can induce you to see yourself enjoying or profiting from the benefits I've promised you, it's a very short step to your wanting them. It's as simple as that. That's why the ads say so often, "Just *imagine yourself* behind the wheel of this beautiful, traffic-stopping, 220HP Puma GT!"

IMPARTING CONVICTION.   There is a psychological phenomenon called cognitive dissonance which is discomfort caused by *two* conflicting thoughts. In a buying situation, people are often beset by doubts and fears because before and after making a buying decision, an uncomfortable dissonance is set up. A little mental bell goes off that says, "Are you sure you are making the right decision?"

Knowing this, the salesperson is careful to supply the assurance that the buy decision is a wise one. Often people long for some kind of rationalization that will make them feel better. "Of course it's high-priced, but think of all the hours of pleasure you are going to get out of it." Salespeople supply warranties (double your money back), testimonials, before-and-after pictures, scientific proof, and "Mrs. Smith down the street just bought one" to lessen a consumer's doubts.

ASKING FOR THE ORDER.   It is an axiom of sales that you never walk away from the prospect without asking for the order. The decision can only go for or against you and the odds are 2 to 1. If you allow a prospect to stall ("I think I better talk to my wife about it"), the odds against you are far greater. So salespeople ask, "Will you have two scoops or one?" "Is it cash or charge?" "Will you want me to install it?" "Please sign here to confirm the order." There are many, many more— and the good salesperson continually uses them.

14

Acres of Diamonds:
Industrial Selling

INDUSTRIAL VS. CONSUMER—
THIRTEEN VITAL DIFFERENCES

THE CONSUMER. The big brewers, cigarette makers, coffee and tea sellers deal with millions of people every day. A big industrial manufacturer may have only a dozen or so customers. A cereal manufacturer never meets or gets to know most of the people who eat his cereal. But an industrial manufacturer is quite apt to know his customers on a first-name basis.

The customer for consumer goods buys on a basis of personal preference and decision while the purchase of industrial goods often depends on the opinion of several people. Most important, the purchaser of industrial goods is a professional buyer whose standards and attitudes are quite different from those of a person buying something for himself.

THE MARKET SEGMENT.   Because the industrial manufacturer has fewer customers and knows them far more intimately than does the manufacturer of consumer goods, his market segments are often much easier to define. Lockheed Aircraft, for example, knows exactly who its customers are. However, this does not mean that there is no chance for market differentiation and the creation of new market segments. There is just as much opportunity for this among industrial manufacturers as there is among makers of consumer goods, sometimes more.

THE MARKETING ENVIRONMENT.   The industrial manufacturer is likely to feel changes in the economic weather far more sharply and quickly than does the manufacturer of the staples of everyday consumer consumption.

HIGH INTEREST RATES.   These can be an annoyance to individual borrowers. But when climbing interest rates limit home building, the impact is felt quickly and cruelly through a host of manufacturers of wallboard and plumbing supplies, hardware, and lumber.

CONSTRAINTS.   The industrial manufacturer must operate within many of the legal constraints placed upon the maker of consumer goods. In addition, he is faced with the constraints imposed by his own customers in the form of specifications. The industrial manufacturer is held to far higher standards of outside quality control. Makers of consumer goods, of course, have their own quality controls and standards; they operate within the vague limits of "consumer satisfaction."

PRODUCTS.   The industrial purchaser must also look for a need and fill it as in the consumer marketing concept. But in the industrialist's case, the job may be somewhat simplified. As you have discovered, consumers' needs, wants, and desires are often unpredictable and hard to discover. The industrial producer often has customers come to him and ask, "Can you make this for us?" Other times specifications will be offered to him, and he will have an opportunity to decide whether to manufacture the item.

Industrial manufacturers are far less likely than those in consumer goods to find themselves backing the wrong horse. They have a good idea of what their trade can use before they manufacture it. On the other hand, they have the tremendous task of educating their customers in the use of new materials and new products. One instance is the steady stream of organic chemically-based new products that has kept packaging in a constant state of change.

PRICE.   When dealing with professional buyers, the approach to pricing is different than that taken with consumers. For one thing, a contract is usual. This contract is often the result of long and detailed negotiation between buyer and seller. Before settling on a reasonable price, the industrial buyer must consider such factors as delivery dates, rebates, warranties, and technical services.

DISTRIBUTION.   Generally speaking, distribution channels for industrial products are shorter and less complicated than those for consumer goods. Many industrial products go directly from the manufacturer to the user. A builder of automotive generators will have a contract with an automobile manufacturer and will ship his product directly from his factory to the automobile assembly plant. On the other hand, some dealers in industrial products are actually middlemen. Garage mechanics can buy automobile parts from auto supply houses as can individuals who wish to work on their own cars. Steel companies for structural steel parts are often independent middlemen who perform a warehousing and delivery service for builders within a certain area.

PACKAGING.   If you ship steel beams, you have no packaging problem. But, for most industrial marketers, packaging presents a real functional problem. Protection and shipping weight are prime considerations. Often the packaging must be tailormade for individual products. How do you package a giant generator so that it will arrive undamaged? How do you pack a delicately adjusted and calibrated piece of scientific equipment?

PROMOTION.   Industrial promotion is not only a whole new ballgame compared to consumer promotion, but is, for most of us, an *unknown* ballgame. Few are aware of the sheer volume of industrial advertising aside from all other forms of promotion. Few of us ever get a chance to read trade publications such as *Coal Age, Game Bird Breeders, Pheasant Farmers,* and *Agricultural Gazette,* yet there are hundreds of these publications. There is practically no trade or industry in the United States, from beekeeping to ocean floor mining and exploration, that does not have at least one publication devoted to its interests. (And, as new industries are born, new publications that carry their advertising are born, too.)

PRINTED PROMOTIONAL MATERIAL.   This literature has a very important place in industrial promotion. Frequently they are elaborate and expensive jobs with 4-color photographs and technical renderings printed on high-gloss stock.

The selection of industrial products often requires long, serious consideration. Thousands of dollars are involved and decisions are rendered at several executive levels. The industrial seller should place effective literature covering his products in as many key decisionmakers' hands as possible. Industrial salespeople cannot always have as much time with key executives as they would like; the colorful, carefully rendered product brochure can take up much of the slack.

SELLING.   Today, the consumer salesperson tends to exert less and less effect on buying decisions. The tremendous growth in supermarkets and other self-help stores is making the salesclerk obsolete in many cases. In industrial selling, however, salespeople continue to occupy a key position. Part of their job is to have very deep insight into their client's operation. Frequently the manufacturer's representative is an engineer or possesses a technical skill. Obviously, the salesperson calling on physicians, oil drillers, valve manufacturers, and aircraft firms has to speak their language.

As a result, many industrial customers lean on their supplier-salespeople for advice, help, and expertise. The relationship between buyer and seller becomes a far closer one than is the case with consumer selling.

THE BUYER.   The industrial buyer regards the salesperson in a different and more important light than is the case in consumer goods. In industry, the terms supplier and sales rep become synonymous. The supplier is vital to the buyer and his company. They need each other, and sometimes the buyer's needs are greatest. Buyers keep a file of suppliers and maintain good working relations with all of them. He or she never knows when a situation may arise in which a part or product may be needed in a hurry. Also, the time may come when the buyer must ask the seller to take back an order.

IDENTIFYING INDUSTRIAL PRODUCTS AND SERVICES

Who Is Industry's Consumer Market?

So far we have defined industrial to be products used by people who make the things that other people buy. As an example, we used an automobile and its parts contributed by many manufacturers. But this industrial market may be far deeper and broader than you think. For instance, a baker makes bread that the consumer buys. The industrial manufacturer who supplies him is a miller who makes and markets flour in commercial quantities.

What about the owner of the grain elevator who sold the wheat to the miller? And what about the farm supply store that sold the seed, fertilizer, and tractor to the farmer? Your one loaf of bread involved literally dozens of industrial manufacturers. This is why total industrial sales volume far exceeds that of consumer sales. Let's look at some of the categories of users of industrial equipment and the kinds of things they buy.

FARMERS, MINERS, FISHERMEN.   These are people who, in a sense, reap the benefits of nature. The farmer, as we have just seen, must buy seed and fertilizer and farm equipment. The mining and oil and gas industries depend on various kinds of drilling equipment as well as specialized materials and moving and handling equipment. Fishermen are dependent on the design and manufacture of various kinds of draggers and trawlers. They also need nets and navigational equipment.

CONSTRUCTION.   Builders of buildings, bridges, and highways have their own needs for industrial goods. Giant cranes tower over every new construction site. Tons of structural steel shapes must be purchased.

MANUFACTURERS.   From the automobile maker to the manufacturer of paper clips, they all depend on someone, whether a builder of generators or a maker of steel wire.

THE TRANSPORTATION NETWORK AND PUBLIC UTILITIES. Giant generators must be purchased and installed before electric power can flow. Think of all the miles of copper wire the telephone companies must purchase and use. Without specialized fuels and lubricants our transportation systems of ships, planes, trucks, and trains would come to a halt.

WHOLESALERS AND RETAILERS.   Specialized materials-handling equipment is used in modern warehouses. And just think of all the furnishings it takes to open a retail store—mannequins, display cases, lighting equipment, elevators, and escalators.

CITY, STATE, AND FEDERAL GOVERNMENTS.   Probably the greatest industrial consumers of all are governmental agencies. How many gallons of printer's ink, how many reams of paper do they use? A new guided-missile system is an industrial purchase as are snow plows and street-sweeping equipment, fleets of police cars, and policemen's badges.

THE PURCHASING AGENT—
A CAT OF A DIFFERENT COLOR

If you were to walk into the reception room at the main office of a grocery chain, you would find that it was sizable and well furnished with comfortable chairs and couches. The room would be well-lit, and there would be reading material, much of it trade, on a coffee table. Indeed, there might be a coffee percolator going. The receptionists would be efficient and friendly and address most of the people in the room by their names. There will be one or two phones available to those who must make an outside call. When the receptionist says, "Mr. Smith, Mr. Jones will see you now," Smith knows he is going in to see a knowledgeable specialist. If Mr. Smith represents a Midwest meat packer and processer, he knows he will be talking to the meat buyer. If he were from a bakery, he would do his selling to the buyer of bakery products.

The specialized buyer is typical of most big industries today. Modern industry has become so complex and technology has made such giant strides that industrial purchasing has focused on narrower and narrower areas.

Let us look at some of the roles the purchasing agent and his department play.

The Purchasing Agent as Planner

One of the buyer's most important functions is anticipating company needs and making plans for meeting them. This can be a very complex process in which all phases of the business must work together.

Ensuring that there will be enough lumber to meet the plant's orders for door and window frames requires planning and negotiation —and maybe a little crystal ball-gazing. But what about the shipyard contracting a nuclear submarine or the firm contracting a spaceship destined for the moon? Within a definite time frame (possibly contractually imposed), the buyer must secure and schedule literally thousands of items for delivery.

The PERT Chart

The Program Evaluation Review Technique was conceived during the construction of the Polaris missile. These flow charts of interlocking events simply could not work without the purchasing department playing a key role. Here, for example, is a list of 13 events in a PERT flowchart for building an airplane. This is a very simple one. The events were:

1. Program go-ahead.
2. Initiate engine procurement.
3. Complete plans and specifications.
4. Complete fuselage drawings.
5. Submit G.F.A.E. (government furnished airplane equipment) requirements.
6. Award tail assembly contract.
7. Award wings contract.
8. Complete manufacture of fuselage.
9. Complete assembly of fuselage—engine.
10. Receive wings from subcontractors.
11. Receive tail assembly from subcontractors.
12. Receive G.F.A.E.
13. Complete aircraft.

You can see how many of these key events the purchasing department was directly concerned with.

The Purchasing Agent as Source Developer

There is a supplier's file in every purchasing department. This is sometimes a simple card file, but in other cases, may be far more elaborate, containing a detailed record of the purchaser's relationship with that particular supplier.

It is in the purchasing agent's best interests to have available a number of dependable known suppliers. For this reason, alert purchasing agents go out of their way not only to discover dependable sources of supply, but also to develop them when necessary. A purchasing agent may award an experimental contract simply to work with and learn about a new potential source.

Earlier the reception room of the home office of a big food chain was described. Treating your suppliers well is indicative of another important attitude of purchasing agents: the cultivation of a long-term, comfortable relationship with their suppliers is crucial.

Industrial buyers are not simply people who are trying to get the best buy for their employers. Nor are industrial salespeople out to sell the limit. Both are involved in a long-term association of mutual benefit.

This brings us to reciprocity, the "I'll scratch your back if you'll scratch mine" principle. There is nothing inherently wrong or evil about reciprocity. It is the natural tendency of a company to do business with people who do business with them. If you are the president of a truck line serving the citrus business, you don't drink tomato juice for breakfast.

INDUSTRIAL PROMOTION—HOW A POSTAGE STAMP CAN MAKE A MILLION DOLLAR DEAL

Among the big Madison Avenue agencies that serve the multimillion-dollar national advertisers, an industrial account is as rare as the whooping crane. There's a good reason for this. In comparison with the nationally-distributed consumer items advertiser, the industrial advertiser spends very little on print advertising. Readership of his trade magazine is small, and space costs are low. It's just not economically feasible for the big agencies to handle the account. A small, obscure agency can do a great job for the industrial client; pick up a trade magazine and take a look.

An industrial budget is usually spent on print advertising placed in trade magazines for industries the advertiser wishes to reach. Radio and television are not usually considered because they cannot segment the industrial advertiser's market properly.

Unlike the consumer-goods advertiser, the industrial company is likely to spend far more for literature such as brochures and booklets. Many of these are remarkably elaborate. They are printed on high-gloss paper, with four-color photography and elaborate diagrams and charts.

These brochures are an important part of industrial promotion, and they are essential to industrial marketing. An industrial salesperson's product is often a complicated one. His sales story and problem-solving approach require time, too. Frequently he or she may anticipate a number of calls on account before the decision stage is reached. The brochure, therefore, must act as "the salesperson you leave behind." It makes it possible for the call to be shortened to a reasonable time, because the customer has a chance to study the brochure at his leisure. As a result, the customer is better prepared to listen and comprehend at the next sales call, and the salesperson has been aided in getting his or her story across in an interesting, logical, and convincing way.

The common business letter, however, can often turn out to be the industrial promotor's best friend. This is not a form letter with a taped address on it, but a personal letter from one executive to another. Business executives, small business executives particularly, read their mail carefully. Here are some writing tips:

1. Write in plain, unadorned English.
2. Be sure you have something important to say to your prospect.
3. Say it clearly and simply.
4. Ask for action. Leave the door open for a follow-up.

A letter offers tremendous sales possibilities for the small businessperson who masters its use. If you don't feel you can write this kind of letter yourself, get some professional help.

Letters are the least expensive promotion device yet they can bring in business out of proportion to their cost. Here's just one example:

Joe Shuster was an experienced auto mechanic who had established his own truck maintenance business. His customers were small fleet operators who couldn't afford a full-time maintenance man. Joe had many friends around town in the repair and parts business. When a fleet was having trouble with constant breakdowns, Joe was pretty sure to hear about it. Then he'd sit down and write the troubled fleet owner a letter describing his services and offering to eliminate the headaches. Joe says his letters have brought him as much business as he can handle.

15

The Marketing Program: Putting It All Together

Let us review some of the things we have learned and recall some of the places we have been so far in marketing. You are going to meet some old friends as we call each one up to play his appointed role in the great drama that is about to unfold.

You are aware that there is such a thing as a modern marketing concept—a way of looking at marketing in which consumer satisfaction and consumer needs play the important role.

You've seen that the consumer is motivated by a number of different forces; that he can be grouped or segmented in a number of different ways, and the characteristics of these segments or target models can be closely identified or "profiled."

You know that, out there in the marketplace, there are a number of forces swirling around—some of them fairly controllable, others not so controllable. Of the more controllable factors, you have a good grasp of the parts played by Price, Product, Distribution, Promotion, and Packaging.

You have also seen that there are a variety of methods by which we can gather information needed to help make decisions—both from within the company and outside it. Now we are going to narrow our focus and put the spotlight directly on the marketing manager himself as he makes his contribution to the broad marketing goals of his company.

You will be treading some fairly familiar pathways—until we arrive at that exciting and scary place where you are going to have to put your reputation, and maybe your future, on the line!

PLANNING IS A PROCESS

A plan must come before all else. This is a well-established principle of management, including marketing management. A plan sets goals, describes the way the goals will be achieved, and gives a certain amount of control over events. Planning is a process in which we first try to see the situation as it really is and then determine what realistic goals are. Methods are formulated for reaching goals (including alternative methods), and means for measuring progress toward the goals are set. Progress is assessed so adjustments can be made as necessary.

Marketing plans have all these characteristics. In addition, marketing plans are both long-term and short-term. A plan might be deliberately designed to meet a temporary situation or to be in effect only between certain dates. Marketing plans can also be long-term and short-term within themselves. Some elements of a marketing plan may last for the life of the company, "the customer is always right" policy, for example. Price structures are not lightly changed either and may continue for a number of years. Promotion policies, on the other hand, can be, and often are, changed overnight. Production changes dictated by style or new designs can also bring short-range elements into planning.

In Chapter 7 the steps to be taken when a new product is conceived and prepared for the launch were described. Let's start from that point. The product has been successful on the test market. You are ready to proceed.

You have learned much about the strategies and tactics for product, price, packaging, promotion, and distribution. You have seen how these operate individually. Now it is time for you, the marketing manager, to shape them into a unified, working whole.

THE FIVE DECISION POINTS

There are a number of factors that, singly or in combination, are going to have a bearing on your strategy decisions.

1. *The Type of Product.* Products can be classified by consumer reaction toward them. Thus, we have convenience goods such as milk, cigarettes, newspapers, and items on our regular grocery shopping list. We pick them up where we see them, often by impulse. Price isn't a great factor (even in the food store we can anticipate the cost at the checkout counter), and little planning goes into our purchase.

Shopping goods are products we are willing to shop around for. We examine differences in features and prices. Larger homes, cars, washing machines, and furniture fall into this category.

Specialty goods are items we are willing to go to some trouble to locate. We are also willing to pay a premium for them. Art objects and other collectors' items, especially designer clothes and prestige labels, fall into this class.

You can see how decisions about the marketing mix would be affected under these varying circumstances. In the case of convenience goods, intensive distribution is a necessity. Promotion may not be a factor (Hershey chocolate bars were not advertised for years). Price becomes high stablized.

Shopping goods place heavy emphasis on product features, quality, and innovations. The type of retail outlet becomes important, and retail cooperation both in advertising and personal selling becomes a factor.

Specialty goods may require specialized advertising in particular media. They offer opportunities for high profit margins. Good, continuous promotion is important.

2. *Business Conditions.* The state of business can have very bad effects on your marketing strategy. A recession, resulting in tight money, brings home and apartment building to a virtual standstill. Manufacturers of lumber, roofing, insulation, bathroom fixtures, and hardware have to alter their marketing strategies drastically.

3. *Competition.* You want to know how much competition there is and what it is doing. Is the market overcrowded with companies with a firm hold on their market segments? Are they old and complacent and ready to be taken by a new product? Do you have an innovation that will put them all in the backseat?

4. *Your Target Markets.* Of vital consideration will be your target markets that you have defined and profiled. Market segmentation is particularly important in new product introduction. Under the modern market concept, firms often search for consumer needs, then design the product to fit them. Ideally your product will fill an unanswered need. Segmentation allows you to match up the need and the product. It makes it possible for you to get to know the character of your segment intimately. You may discover, too, that you have more than one segment—each of which are loyal to your product for different reasons.

5. *Stage in the Product Life Cycle.* New and revised marketing strategies must be worked out regularly for all the products in the company line. Sometimes marketing strategies for a particular product will change little, year after year. But as a product enters a new phase in its life cycle, fresh strategic thinking must be applied.

THE FIVE "P'S"— AND HOW YOU JUGGLE THEM

Each of the P's brings areas of opportunity. Your job is to make specific decisions in each area and then fit them together in a smoothly operating whole. There is no magic formula for doing this; there is no infallible grid or model. But there are some devices that can help you.

Here are some of the opportunity areas in which you will be able to make "mix" decisions.

PRODUCT.   You may introduce a completely new product to your line. You may add some significantly different features or improvements. You may come up with a different service policy or more extensive guarantees.

DISTRIBUTION.   You may decide upon a different mode of transportation. You could decide to eliminate a certain type of middleman or substitute another. You might alter the concept of the kind and number of retail outlets you hope to use. You might change your inventory system.

PACKAGING.   You could introduce a new label design. A new pack might be introduced (such as the six-pack). You could adopt a completely new material. You could go into new sizes or have a new shipping container designed.

PRICE.   A new discount or allowance structure could be set up. You may have to make a choice between a high skimming price or a lower penetration price. Your decision could be to lower prices in an effort to increase production.

PROMOTION.   You may decide to let a new advertising agency handle your account. You may call for tests of the effectiveness of advertising themes and techniques. Your in-store promotional material could be redesigned completely.

Let's use the five areas of decision-making just mentioned. How can you test each so the odds for success are in your favor as much as possible? What can you do to be as certain as possible that you are making the right choice to feed into the marketing mix? Let's take them a step at a time.

PRODUCT. If your product is something people put in their mouths, you will certainly gather a panel and let members taste the product. A use test of a sample of your segment universe will tell you if you are on the right track or warn you against a problem you should fix.

DISTRIBUTION. Remember the trade-offs discussed in the chapter on distribution? Here's a chance to run cost analyses and other tests to determine the most profitable means of transportation and distribution. This includes break-bulk decisions and warehouse locations, all of which can be the subject of statistical analysis.

PACKAGING. Package design plays an important part in the success or failure of your marketing mix. Fortunately you can determine through research reactions of consumers to your colors and designs. It is also possible to measure consumers' and distribution channel members' reactions to new packs, sizes, and closures.

PRICE. One of the basic tools used by the marketing manager in arriving at the right price, the break-even point calculated through break-even analysis, has been covered. We also touched on marginal analysis, another popular tool available in price-setting.

PROMOTION. Advertising results are always a controversial issue. The answer to the question "How well will my promotional efforts perform for me?" is vital to your success. It is possible for you to get indications of the effectiveness of both selling appeals and advertising techniques, as well as media selection before your money is committed. The split run with a hidden offer or coupon is a test often used in advertising. There are several methods to pretest television commercials. Your agency's media director should be able to supply you with a well-reasoned and statistically accurate analysis of your proposed media expenditures. All media—newspapers, TV, and so on—have carefully researched materials on their audiences.

In the goal-setting phase of planning, forecasting and premising play important roles. You should understand the difference between the two. *Forecasts* are estimates of what is going to happen. *Premises* are planning assumptions based on these forecasts. Those involved in planning must use and understand consistent planning premises to achieve the greatest degree of coordination.

The sales forecast is a cornerstone in market planning. We are saying, "If we do things this way, what are the sales results likely to be?" But others are saying, "Can we afford to do things this way if these are the results you think we are going to get?" So, to a great extent, your sales forecast will dictate your mode and extent of operation.

In calculating sales potential, market factors must be taken into consideration. A *market factor* is something you can measure that will play a part in determining your sales. My morning paper carries a story about how the "baby boom" of the war years is affecting real estate sales. That's a market factor. There is a *correlation* here that will be mentioned later. When you convert this measurable factor into a decimal or percentage that will be used in your formula, it is referred to as an *index*.

You are also going to refer to market potential in making your sales forecast. The *market potential* is the total available sales existing for that particular type of product during a particular state of the economy—for example, the number of tubes of toothpaste sold in the U.S. last year.

You will also be interested in getting a figure for your *market penetration*. This asks, "How big a piece of the potential market are we likely to be able to bite off?" This was previously referred to as share of market.

Forecasting Methods

The first method, the chain ratio method, is basically a calculation based on subdivisions of marketing factors, starting with the largest and fractioning to your estimated market (number of babies of diaperable age × number of diapers used per baby × percentage of users of disposable diapers).

Another model is the market buildings method. In this you rely on the Standard Industrial Classification System (S.I.C.) based on the

U.S. Census of Manufacturers. If you manufacture coffins, you might want to know how many funeral directors there were in a given territory and the number of funerals they handled last year.

Forecasting for Future Demand

Forecasting the theoretical potential market for your product works from known statistical factors often based on past performance. But forecasting future demand for a given product, actual demand, is somewhat more difficult. Kotler has described it as "the art of anticipating what buyers are likely to do under a given set of conditions."[1]

The Consumer-Intention-To-Buy Survey is one method to obtain future demand figures. These surveys are generally carried out by professional organizations. The more expensive, larger, and less frequent the purchase, the more accurate this method is likely to be.

Salesforce and dealer estimates are frequently relied upon. This is less scientific than a properly done Intention-To-Buy Survey, but it is practical, expert testimony taken directly from the firing line. But, there are certain drawbacks. Dealers may be overly optimistic—a natural and commendable state—or sales personnel may hesitate to make a commitment they may have trouble living up to later.

Companies often rely on the opinions of outside experts in estimating future sales. They may subscribe to newsletters in their field. Consultations with editorial staffs of trade magazines can be helpful. Larger companies sometimes have a panel of experts come in, examine the sales opportunity, and develop a pool of estimates of future sales.

Market Targeting

As mentioned earlier, one of the important considerations affecting your marketing program will be the character of your market segmentation. Here we must distinguish between *differentiated* and *undifferentiated* marketing. Sellers of certain products do not differentiate their markets at all. Chiquita Banana speaks to all of us as do the Orange Juice producers from Florida. Their marketing mix problems are much simpler because of this lack of differentiation of markets.

Others, however, see themselves as appealing to a number of different market segments and doing it profitably. Car makers, distillers, even the cigarette manufacturers, make a variety of products to satisfy various market segments. This is the genesis of the product line.

[1] Philip Kotler, *Marketing Management, Analysis, Planning, and Control*, 3rd ed. (Englewood Cliffs, N.J.: Prentice-Hall, Inc., 1976), p. 129.

Today many companies have adopted this concept of differentiated marketing. What it means to market planning is this: your job is not one of just identifying the needs and character of a market segment and designing a marketing plan to fit it; it is one of recognizing the needs and character of different market segments and tailoring and coordinating your marketing plans for each within the realities of costs and income.

As this is written, there are two TV commercials being run by the same brewery: one for their regular beer, the other for their premium. The regular beer commercial features longshoremen coming off the job at the end of the day and gathering at a dingy waterfront bar. The other, for the premium, shows a group of well-dressed young businessmen seated in what is obviously an expensive, big city restaurant. Two beer markets—but poles apart!

EVALUATION—THE BOTTOM LINE

The final step in the marketing plan is evaluation. It asks the questions "What did we do right?" and "What did we do wrong?"

First, a word about evaluations. Evaluations are commonly used for a variety of functions. The U.S. Navy, for example, constantly evaluates its personnel and promotes or retires on a basis of these evaluations. Two factors have to be kept in mind no matter what is being evaluated. Evaluations are difficult to make and are subject to wide variations.[2] Evaluations should not be used for punitive purposes, but rather for improving performance.

The marketing audit is an extensive—and expensive—form of evaluation. It is an appraisal of the total and individual performances carried out by a company in the marketing effort. The problem is who makes the appraisal and with what instruments. But, as Kotler states, "Unfortunately, the marketing audit has not yet developed into a standard tool comparable to the financial audit."[3]

Whether the extensive market audit is used or a combination of gross sales by units, sales dollars, or share of market, the marketing manager is looking for soft spots in the plan. One of the first places he looks is the popular 80-20 concept. This theory states that 80% of sales can usually be attributed to 20% of customers. It is true in any business that customers range from very active to very inactive. The job is to determine at what cut-off point the small, expensive-to-sell customer

[2] See Mental Measurements Year Book, A.C. Buros, ed. (Gryphon Press—1, Highland Park, N.J., 1972).

[3] Kotler, op. cit.

should be abandoned so that further efforts can be made at the more profitable end of the sales.

What really concerns the evaluators and marketing managers is this: It is practically impossible to correlate sales or income and the expenditures for individual efforts within the marketing mix. William J. Stanton has put it quite neatly:

> If a company spends $250,000 more on advertising this year, management ordinarily cannot state what the increase in sales volume or profits should be. Nor do the executives know what the results would have been if an equivalent sum had been devoted to product development, management training seminars for middlemen, or some other aspect of the marketing program.[4]

This brings us back to where we started. It is a long and costly job to get answers to the big questions . . . it is easier and less expensive to get answers to the smaller ones . . . and the little answers add up to the big answers.

PUTTING THE PROGRAM TOGETHER

We have established the reasons for a plan, and you have seen the mechanics of a planning process. You are aware of the part that forecasting plays in planning.

You are also aware that there are certain internal and external factors that you must take into account when drawing up the plan. These are such things as the current state of your product, its competitive position in relation to others, general business conditions, and the kinds of markets you have targeted for your product.

Further, we are well aware of the five great areas of flexibility—the mix of product, price, distribution, promotion, and packaging. To a great extent, these are the blocks with which our marketing strategy will be built.

Finally, you recognize that it is through testing and information-gathering that it is possible to reduce the odds against success.

Now, knowing these things, how are you going to react when the time comes for you to submit a marketing program for your particular product?

"GOALS DOWN—PLANS UP."   In most cases, you will be alerted to the need for a new marketing plan by the corporate execu-

---

[4] William J. Stanton, *Fundamentals of Marketing*, 5th ed., (N.Y.: McGraw-Hill Book Company, 1978), pp. 5–15.

tives of your company. They will be saying to you, in effect, these are our corporate goals for next year. Please send us your product and your department plan to contribute to reaching our goals.

THE PLAN'S FORMAT.   Your reply to this question is, of course, your product marketing plan. The focus of a plan will vary from company to company. Generally speaking, it will consist of the following:

1. A "state of the nation" report on your product, its progress since last heard from, the state of the competition.
2. A projection, based on what has happened, and what you thought might happen, of next year's sales and profits.
3. An outline of what you plan to do in the marketplace next year to enhance your sales and profits picture and how much it will cost.
4. A description of how you will carry out this plan, market it, and keep control of it.

This is the formal plan, in barest outline, as it is prepared in the marketing departments of the largest corporations. But it isn't for big corporations alone. Even if you are a single entrepreneur, you should have one, too, because what goes on *within* the framework of this plan is what you should do if you want your business to succeed.

Remember—success in business is built on the stones of failure. Having studied this book, there should be little doubt in your mind as to how *not* to do a great many things . . .

How *not* to carry out research.
How *not* to look for consumer needs.
How *not* to understand your market segment.
How *not* to price your product properly.
How *not* to promote it properly.
. . . And a hundred other *nots*.

Like a nautical chart, I hope this book has identified for you the shoals and rocks on which so many other businesses have foundered. And like the same chart, I hope it has shown you how to steer the clear, unobstructed course to business success—your safe harbor. Good luck!

Index